CONTENTS

S0-DFL-494

Contact: All inquiries and correspondence should be sent to Indian Chief Publishing House, P.O. Box 1814, Davis, CA 95617, or *info@indianchief.net*.

Book data: The Complete Kauai Guidebook, 3rd edition, ISBN 0-916841-75-8.

Contributors to this book: B. Sangwan, David J. Russ, Kiran Savage-Sangwan

Printed in the U.S.A.

HOW TO USE THIS GUIDEBOOK | Icons and Numbers

HOW TO USE THIS GUIDEBOOK

This guidebook is divided into three chapters: Overview, History, and an *Exploring the Island* chapter entitled Kauai. The *Exploring* chapter is subdivided into sections, areas, segments, and points of interest (see below).

Section: **LIHUE AREA**

Area: **Lihue**

Segment: *Rice Street*

Point of Interest: *Kauai Museum*

What the Icons and Numbers Mean:

This guidebook is sectioned, and entries in it cross-referenced, to enable you to quickly and easily find what you are looking for, a lot like links on web pages on the Internet. And that is where the icons and numbers come in—as a link.

 Icon: This ubiquitous icon is a prod for you to reference a corresponding map for orientation or, if you are already looking at a map in the book, to reference a corresponding section or area where you will find more information.

Numbers are of three different kinds:

1 **Section Reference:** At the start of each section, such as Lihue Area or South Shore, a small island map with a rectangle defining the area covered in the section appears, together with a number that corresponds to the number-coded section on the larger island map at the start of the chapter. This is designed to enable you to reference the section on the map for orientation and an overview.

Entries Between Rules: Also, where sections are lengthier, a list of areas covered in the section appears between parallel rules directly beneath the section heading. This is designed to enable you to quickly find the area relevant to your interest.

2 **Area Reference:** At the start of most areas, such as Wailua or Poipu, a gray box with a number appears. This corresponds to the number-coded area map relevant to the text. This is designed to orient you with the area.

3 **Point of Interest Reference:** Alongside several entries in the book, a black box with a number appears in the side bar. This corresponds to the point of interest located on the referenced area map (described above, in Area Reference). This will enable you to find the relevant points of interest quickly and easily.

▶ *Arrows:* An arrow in the side bar alongside an entry indicates a point of interest that is not referenced on a map.

Alternatively, if you choose to use this book as a traditional guidebook, a quick and easy way into it is the *Index* at the end.

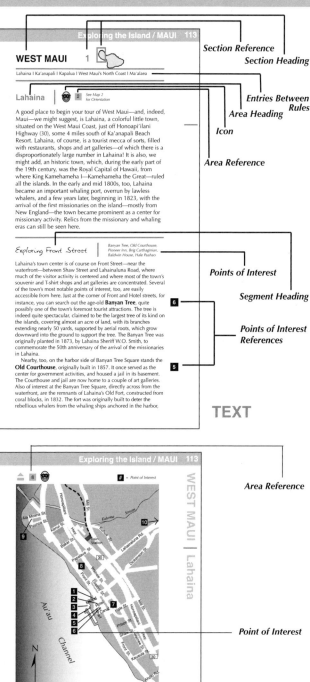

HOW TO USE THIS GUIDEBOOK | Icons and Numbers

TEXT

Exploring the Island / MAUI 113

WEST MAUI 1

Section Reference

Section Heading

Lahaina I Ka'anapali I Kapalua I West Maui's North Coast I Ma'alaea

Lahaina 2 *See Map 2 for Orientation*

Entries Between Rules

Area Heading

Icon

Area Reference

A good place to begin your tour of West Maui—and, indeed, Maui—we might suggest, is Lahaina, a colorful little town, situated on the West Maui Coast, just off Honoapi'ilani Highway (30), some 4 miles south of Ka'anapali Beach Resort. Lahaina, of course, is a tourist mecca of sorts, filled with restaurants, shops and art galleries—of which there is a disproportionately large number in Lahaina! It is also, we might add, an historic town, which, during the early part of the 19th century, was the Royal Capital of Hawaii, from where King Kamehameha I—Kamehameha the Great—ruled all the islands. In the early and mid 1800s, too, Lahaina became an important whaling port, overrun by lawless whalers, and a few years later, beginning in 1823, with the arrival of the first missionaries on the island—mostly from New England—the town became prominent as a center for missionary activity. Relics from the missionary and whaling eras can still be seen here.

Exploring Front Street | *Banyan Tree, Old Courthouse, Pioneer Inn, Brig Carthaginian, Baldwin House, Hale Paahao*

Points of Interest

Segment Heading

Lahaina's town center is of course on Front Street—near the waterfront—between Shaw Street and Lahainaluna Road, where much of the visitor activity is centered and where most of the town's souvenir and T-shirt shops and art galleries are concentrated. Several of the town's most notable points of interest, too, are easily accessible from here. Just at the corner of Front and Hotel streets, for instance, you can search out the age-old **Banyan Tree**, quite possibly one of the town's foremost tourist attractions. The tree is indeed quite spectacular, claimed to be the largest tree of its kind on the islands, covering almost an acre of land, with its branches extending nearly 50 yards, supported by aerial roots, which grow downward into the ground to support the tree. The Banyan Tree was originally planted in 1873, by Lahaina Sheriff W.O. Smith, to commemorate the 50th anniversary of the arrival of the missionaries in Lahaina.

Points of Interest References 6

Nearby, too, on the harbor side of Banyan Tree Square stands the **Old Courthouse**, originally built in 1857. It once served as the center for government activities, and housed a jail in its basement. The Courthouse and jail are now home to a couple of art galleries. Also of interest at the Banyan Tree Square, directly across from the waterfront, are the remnants of Lahaina's Old Fort, constructed from coral blocks, in 1832. The fort was originally built to deter the rebellious whalers from the whaling ships anchored in the harbor,

5

Exploring the Island / MAUI 113

Area Reference

8

– Point of Interest

WEST MAUI | Lahaina

Point of Interest

N

Miles
0   0.5

LAHAINA

Corresponding
MAP

OVERVIEW

The Islands | Getting There | Getting Around | Tourist Information

The Islands

The Hawaiian islands lie approximately 2,400 miles southwest of the west coast of mainland USA, smack in the middle of the Pacific Ocean. The archipelago includes well over a hundred atolls, reefs, shoals and tiny islands spread out over some 1,600 miles of ocean, but there are only eight major islands in the chain: Oahu, Hawaii (the Big Island), Maui, Molokai, Lanai, Kaho'olawe, Kauai and Ni'ihau.

In this book, we cover the island of Kauai (and peripherally Ni'ihau, which is essentially inaccessible to visitors).

See Map 1
for Orientation

Kauai is Hawaii's "Garden Isle," and the northernmost and fourth largest island in the Hawaiian archipelago, encompassing 558 square miles. It comprises a single volcanic land mass, with its highest point more or less at the center of the island. The island is situated approximately 95 miles northwest of Oahu and 17½ miles east-northeast of Ni'ihau.

Kauai has a population of more than 32,000, and is a premier tourist destination, drawing in excess of 1.5 million visitors annually. It has no fewer than 7,000 hotel rooms and rental condominium accommodations, well over a hundred restaurants, and offers a wealth of recreational opportunities, including swimming, snorkeling, scuba diving, surfing, windsurfing, sailing, biking, hiking, horseback riding, golfing and beachcombing. It also boasts a supremely enjoyable, temperate climate, with temperatures ranging from 60°F in January to around 85°F in August.

See Map 11
for Orientation

Ni'ihau is the "Forbidden Isle," privately owned and forbidden to visitors and even Hawaiians who are not residents of the island. It is also the smallest of the eight major Hawaiian islands, 18 miles long and 6 miles wide, comprising all of 72 square miles. The island lies 17½ miles west-northwest of Kauai.

Ni'ihau is fairly flat, arid, and easily the driest island in the state, receiving, on the average, no more than 25-30 inches of rainfall a year. Its mainstay is cattle ranching.

Getting There | *Airports and Airlines*

The good thing about going to Kauai is that you have the option of either flying there directly, non-stop, from mainland USA, or traveling through the busy hub at Honolulu International Airport on the island of Oahu, and from there on an inter-island flight to Kauai. There are also inter-island flights between Honolulu, Oahu, and Kauai, and Maui and Kauai.

Airports

Kauai has two airports: at Lihue (on Kauai's southeast corner), which is the island's principal airport, and a smaller one at Princeville, on the island's north shore.

Airport Contact:
Lihue International Airport, Lihue, Kauai; (808) 246-1448

Traveling Direct to Kauai

The following airlines fly direct to Kauai from the continental U.S.:

Delta Airlines (800) 221-1212/*www.delta.com*
Hawaiian Airlines (800) 882-8811/*www.hawaiianair.com*
United Airlines (800) 864-8331/241-6522/*www.united.com*

Traveling Via Honolulu

Domestic Airlines flying to Honolulu:

American Airlines (800) 433-7300/*www.aa.com*
America West Airlines (800) 235-9292/*www.americawest.com*
Delta Airlines (800) 221-1212/*www.delta.com*
Hawaiian Airlines (800) 882-8811/*www.hawaiianair.com*
Northwest Airlines (800) 225-2525/*www.nwa.com*
United Airlines (800) 864-8331/241-6522/*www.united.com*

International Airlines flying to Honolulu:

Air New Zealand (800) 262-1234/*www.airnewzealand.com*
Air Canada (888) 247-2262/*www.aircanada.com*
China Airlines (800) 227-5118/*www.china-airlines.com*

Japan Airlines (800) 525-3663/*www.jal.co.jp/en*
Korean Air (800) 438-5000/*www.koreanair.com*
Philippines Airlines (800) 435-9725/*www.philippineairlines.com*
Singapore Airlines (800) 742-3333/*www.singaporeair.com*

Inter—Island Flights

There are three Hawaii-based airlines offering daily flights between Honolulu, Oahu, and Kauai. Typically, fares for travel between Honolulu and Kauai range from $85-$105 one-way, to $170-$210 round trip.

Honolulu to Kauai:

Aloha Airlines (808) 244-9071/(800) 367-5250/*www.alohaairlines.com*

Island Air (808) 877-5755/(800) 652-65417(800) 323-3345/ *www.islandair.com*

Hawaiian Airlines (808) 871-6132/(800) 367-5320/882-8811/ *www.hawaiianair.com*

Maui to Kauai (Direct):

Island Air (808) 877-5755/(800) 652-65417(800) 323-3345/ *www.islandair.com*

Getting Around | *Car Rentals, Taxis, Bus*

Taxis are available on the island for point to point travel as well as island tours, and an island-wide bus service links all the population centers along the main routes of travel, from Kekaha on the West Side to Hanalei on the North Shore. But the best and most convenient way to get around the island is still by car, with rentals ranging from around $18-$130 per day to $90-$350 per week.

Car Rentals:

Alamo Rent a Car, Lihue Airport, (808) 246-0645/(800) 327-9633/*www.alamo.com*

Avis Rent a Car, Lihue Airport, (808) 245-3512/(800) 321-3712/831-8000/*www.avis.com*

Budget Car Rental, Lihue Airport, (808) 245-1901/(800) 527-0700/*www.budget.com*

Dollar Car Rental, Lihue Airport, (800) 800-4000/(800) 342-7398/(866) 434-2226/*www.dollar.com*

Hertz Rent a Car, Lihue Airport, (808) 245-3356/(800) 654-3131/654-3011/*www.hertz.com*

National Car Rental, Lihue Airport, (808) 245-5636/(800) 227-7368/*www.nationalcar.com*

Rent a Wreck, (808) 632-0741

Thrifty Rent a Car, Lihue, (808) 246-6252/(800) 367-5238/847-4389/*www.thrifty.com*

Kauai Taxis:

Akiko's, (808) 822-7588; *Bran's Taxi,* (808) 245-6533; *City Cab,* (808) 245-3227; *Kauai Cab Service,* (808) 246-9554; *North Shore Cab & Tours,* (808) 639-7829.

Kauai Bus:

The *Kauai Bus* links Kauai's principal communities around the island, journeying along the main highway, from Kekaha on the West Side to Hanalei on the North Shore. The fare is $1.50 for one-time use, and $15.00 for a monthly pass. A schedule of the route, stops and times can be obtained be obtained by calling them at (808) 241-6410.

Tourist Information

Visitors Bureaus,
Division of Parks and Recreation,
Vacation Rental Agents

Visitors Bureaus

Hawaii Visitors and Convention Bureau (HVCB). Waikiki Business Plaza, 2270 Kalakaua Ave., Suite 801, Honolulu. HI 96815; (808) 923-1811/(800) 464-2924/*www.hvcb.org* or *www.gohawaii. com*. This is Hawaii's principal, one-stop source for visitor information, both for published materials and online information. The "gohawaii" web site has all the reference materials you could want, including listings for accommodations, restaurants, events, tours and recreation. The bureau also offers a free, cover-all publication in its visitor package, *The Islands of Hawaii: A Vacation Planner,* with a wealth of tourist information on places of interest on the islands, recreational opportunities and a wide selection of tours.

Kauai Visitors Bureau (KVB). 4334 Rice St., Suite 101, Lihue, HI 96766; (808) 245-3971/(800) 262-1400/*www.kauaidiscovery.com*; Open 8 a.m.-4.30 p.m., Mon.-Fri. Wealth of tourist information available, including directory of accommodations and restaurants and a calendar of events. Also maps, and Kauai's premier, free tourist publication, *Kauai: A Vacation Planner.* A useful web site for a

Kauai calendar of events is *www.kauaifestivals.com*.

County of Kauai, Office of Tourism. The County of Kauai operates a toll-free, tourist information hotline at (800) 262-1400, available in all 50 states and Canada, 6 a.m.-6 p.m. Mon.-Fri., and 6 a.m.-2 p.m. Sat.-Sun. (Hawaii Standard Time). They also have a useful web site: *www.kauai-hawaii.com*.

Chamber of Commerce

Kauai Chamber of Commerce. 2970 Kele St., Suite 112, Lihue, HI 96766; (808) 245-7363/*www.kauaichamber.org*.; open 8-4.30, Mon.-Fri. Visitor information brochures, including lodging, restaurant and tour company listings.

Division of Parks and Recreation

County of Kauai, Division of Parks and Recreation. 4444 Rice St., Room 150, Lihue, HI 96766; (808) 241-4463. Good source for information and permits for camping in county parks on Kauai.

Department of Land and Natural Resources. State Office Building, 3060 Eiwa St., Room 306, Lihue, HI 96766; (808) 274-3444. Camping permits and information on State Park campgrounds on Kauai.

Vacation Rental Agents

Aloha Rental Management. P.O. Box 1109, Hanalei, HI 96714; (808) 826-7288/(800) 487-9833/*www.800hawaii.com*. One- to four-bedroom condominiums and homes at the Princeville Resort; ocean and golf course views. Rentals range from $115-$300 per day/ $700-$2,100 per week. Minimum stay, 3 nights.

Anini Aloha Properties, Inc. 4270 Kilauea Rd., Ste. I-1, Kilauea, HI 96754; (808) 828-0067/(800) 246-5382/*www.aninialoha.com*. One- to six-bedroom homes and condominium resort accommodations, on the North Shore and Poipu Beach area. Weekly rental rates: $750-$8,500.

Bed & Breakfast Kauai. 6436 Kalama Rd., Kapa'a; (808) 822-1177/(800) 822-1176/*www.bnbkauai.com*. Reservation and referral service for bed and breakfast accommodations on Kauai.

Garden Island Rentals. P.O. Box 57, Koloa, HI 96756; (808) 742-9537/(800) 247-5599/*www.kauairentals.com*. One- to five-bedroom homes and condominium units in the Poipu area, many situated on the beach, with ocean views. Rates from $750-$5,000 per week.

Grantham Resorts. 2721 Poipu Rd., Koloa, HI 96756; (808) 742-7220/(800) 325-5701/*www.grantham-resorts.com*. One- to four-bedroom condominium units and houses, both beachfront and with ocean views, located in the Poipu Beach area. Daily rates from $175-$1,750; weekly rates from $1,200-$9,700. Minimum stay: 3 nights.

Hanalei North Shore Properties. P.O. Box 607, Hanalei, HI 96714; (808) 826-9622/(800) 488-3336/*www.rentalsonkauai.com*. One- to four-bedroom homes and condominiums on Kauai's North Shore; ocean and mountain views. Weekly rates: $525-$8,000.

Kauai Vacation Rentals. 3-3311 Kuhio Hwy., Lihue, HI 96766; (808) 245-8841/(800) 367-5025/*www.kauai-vacation.com*. One- to four-bedroom condominium units and homes, on Kauai's North, East and South shores; many beachfront and oceanview properties. Rental rates range from $85-$1,400 per day to $425-$7,000 per week.

Na Pali Properties. P.O. Box 475, 5-5190 Kuhio Hwy., Hanalei, HI 96714; (808) 826-7272/(800) 715-7273/*www.napaliprop.com*. One- to five-bedroom homes and condominiums, located on the North Shore of Kauai. Several beachfront properties. Rentals range from $85-$1,400 per night, and $425-$5,600 per week.

Oceanfront Realty. P.O. Box 223190, Princeville Center, 5-4280 Kuhio Hwy., Princeville, HI 96722; (808) 826-6585/(800) 222-5541/*www.oceanfrontrealty.com*. One- to four-bedroom condominium units in Princeville, with ocean, mountain and golf course views. Daily rates: $120-$395.

Prosser Realty, Inc. P.O. Box 367, 4379 Rice St., Lihue, HI 96766; (808) 245-4711/(800) 767-4707/*www.prosser-realty.com*. One-, two- and three-bedroom homes and condominium units, located throughout the island; ocean and mountain views. Daily rates: $75-$600; weekly rates: $500-$4,000.

R & R Realty & Rentals. P.O. Box 70, 1661 Pe'e Rd., Poipu, HI 96756; (808) 742-7555/(800) 367-8022/*www.r7r.com*. One- and two-bedroom homes and condominium units, with ocean and mountain views, located in the Poipu Beach area. Rentals range from $100-$300 per day to $600-$1,500 per week. Minimum stay: 4 nights.

Regency Pacific Realty. P.O. Box 223192, Princeville, HI 96722; (808) 826-9775/(800) 826-7782/*www.regencypacificrealty.com*. Oceanview and oceanfront rental units, ranging from studios to two- and three-bedroom homes and condominium apartments and suites. Daily rates: $90-$340.

ReMax Kauai. Princeville Shopping Center, Princeville, HI 96722; (808) 826-9675/(877) 838-8149/*www.remaxkauai.com*.

North Shore and Poipu Beach rental homes, condominium units and villas. Rents range from $110-$850 per day to $770-$6,000 per week.

Rosewood Vacation Rentals. 872 Kamalu Rd., Kapa'a; (808) 822-5216/*www.rosewoodkauai.com*. Country homes and cottages, beach homes, condominium units, apartments, bed and breakfast accommodations, and individual units in a backpacker hostel. Daily rates: $45-$295. Minimum stay, 3 days.

Weather and Time

Weather:

For current weather conditions and forecasts for Kauai, call (808) 245-6001.

Time:

For current Hawaiian Time, call (808) 245-0212.

STORY OF KAUAI | A Brief History

Kauai is Hawaii's oldest island. It began forming nearly 10 million years ago, when a series of eruptions on the ocean floor created a single, shielded volcano. This, with the accumulation of molten lava over a period of time, finally emerged as Mount Wai'ale'ale, 5,148 feet above sea level, at the center of the island. Then, approximately a million years ago, Mount Wai'ale'ale became extinct. In the following years, rivers, streams, ocean waves and the wind sculpted and shaped the island, forming valleys, canyons, cliffs and mountains, notable among them the ancient, deeply eroded Waimea Canyon and the stunning sea cliffs along the Na Pali Coast.

An ancient Hawaiian myth, however, endures that Kauai and the other Hawaiian islands are the offspring of Wakea, the divine embodiment of the sky, and Papa, the earth deity, who arrived in this part of the Pacific from Tahiti. Wakea and Papa first conceived Hawaii, the big island, followed by Maui. Wakea then conceived with Kaulawahine (another deity) the island of Lanai, and with Hina, the island of Molokai. Papa, for her part, thoroughly infuriated, conceived with Lua (a male deity) the island of Oahu. Finally, with all that accomplished, Wakea and Papa reconciled and together conceived Kauai—the most noble of the islands, "born of heavenly quality"—as well as the nearby island of Ni'ihau and its adjoining islets, Lehua and Kaula.

Kauai was also the first Hawaiian island to be inhabited. Its earliest inhabitants were the Marquesans, a Polynesian people who journeyed to Kauai from the Marquesas and Society islands between 500 A.D. and 750 A.D., followed some years later, around 1000 A.D., by the Tahitians. The Marquesans, who journeyed to Hawaii in large outrigger canoes, navigating by the stars across several thousand miles of open ocean, introduced to Kauai and the other Hawaiian islands the first domestic animals, plants and fruit; and the Tahitians, for their part, brought with them their religion and their gods and goddesses, notable among them Kane, the god of all living creatures; Ku, god of war; Pele, goddess of fire; Kaneloa, the god of the land of the departed spirits; and Lono, god of harvest and peace. The Tahitians also introduced to the islands the *kapu* system, a strict social order that affected all aspects of life and formed the core of ancient Hawaiian culture.

According to popular belief, however, the island's first settlers were the *menehune*, Kauai's mysterious little people. The *menehune* were a pixie-like people, around two feet tall, who are credited with several early-day engineering marvels around the island, among them the Alakoko Fishpond and the Menehune Ditch, characteristic in their architecture with interlocking flanged and fitted cut-stone bricks. It is believed that the *menehune* worked only at night, completing entire projects in the course of a single night. Their strength was in their numbers: there are thought to have been so many of them that they could form two rows from Makaweli to Wailua, covering a distance of nearly 30 miles. The *menehune* ultimately left Kauai just as mysteriously as they had arrived, although in a recent census some 53 Hawaiians claimed to be descendants of the *menehune*.

At any rate, the first white man to arrive in Kauai was Captain James Cook, a British explorer in search of a northwest passage from the Pacific Ocean to the Atlantic Ocean. He landed at Waimea, on Kauai's west shore, on January 20, 1778. It was his first landing in the Hawaiian islands. In the following years, others followed, including Nathaniel Portlock and George Dixon, who had served under Cook, and Captain George Vancouver, another British explorer who also landed at Waimea, in March of 1792. These early Europeans, however, also brought with them to the Hawaiian islands the white man's disease. Hawaiians had little or no resistance to Western diseases, and over a period of some 100 years following Cook's first contact with the islands, nearly 80% of Hawaii's indigenous population was wiped out.

The mid and late 1700s also ushered in Hawaii's era of monarchy. Kamehameha I—also known as Kamehameha the Great—was born in the late 1750s, and by 1791 he had gained control of the island of Hawaii. In 1794, following the death of King Kahekili of Maui, he conquered Maui as well as the nearby islands of Lanai and Molokai. The following year, in 1795, Kamehameha also conquered Oahu. His bid to conquer Kauai, however, was thwarted on at least two occasions in 1796, by bad weather and turbulent seas, resulting in his failure to cross the Kauai Channel with his armada. But in 1819, after learning of yet another attempt by Kamehameha to invade Kauai, King Kaumuali'i of Kauai, who had become the ruler of the island in 1796 at the age of 16, ceded Kauai to Kamehameha. And so Kauai became a tributary kingdom of Kamemeha the Great, even though Kaumuali'i was permitted to continue governing the island.

In the early 1800s, too, the first Russians arrived in Kauai. A ship owned by the Russian American Company, an agent of the Russian government engaged in the fur trade, ran aground just off the southwest coast of Kauai; and in 1816, Georg Scheffer, a German in the employ of the Russian company, was sent to secure the goods on the ship. Scheffer, once ashore, built at the mouth of the Waimea River, near the early settlement of Waimea, a Russian fort, and named it Fort Elizabeth, for Czarina Elizabeth, wife of Alexander I. The Russian presence on the island was nevertheless short-lived, for the fort was soon abandoned by Scheffer.

The 1820s brought to the Hawaiian islands the first missionaries. The earliest on Kauai were Samuel and Mercy Whitney, who arrived in Waimea in 1820 to establish a mission. The Whitneys were followed by others: in 1828, Peter Gulick arrived in Waimea, and some years later, in 1835, he established the Koloa Mission in nearby Koloa; in 1834, William Alexander journeyed to Hanalei, on Kauai's north shore, and established the Waioli Mission; and in 1841, Father Walsh, a Catholic priest, established the first Catholic mission in Koloa, then went on to build, in 1856, the nearby St. Raphael's Church. Among other notable early-day missionaries were George Rowell, who arrived in Waimea in 1846 and built there the Gulick House, the Great Stone Church and the Waimea Hawaiian Church; and Abner and Lucy Wilcox, who lived and worked at the mission in Hanalei during the late 1800s.

The year 1835 witnessed the birth of Hawaii's sugar industry at Koloa, on Kauai's south shore. The first sugar plantation and mill were established that year at Koloa by William Hooper of Honolulu-based Ladd & Company. Other sugar plantations followed: at Lihue in 1849, at the Grove Farm, near Lihue, in 1864, and at Kekaha in 1898. Thus, sugar became the island's principal industry for the next nearly 150 years, until it was finally displaced by tourism. However, a vestige of Kauai's sugar industry, the old Lihue Sugar Mill, built in 1849, is still in operation, processing more than 65,000 tons of sugar annually.

The late 1800s and early 1900s also brought to the Hawaiian islands waves of immigrants—mostly Chinese, Japanese, Filipino, Portugese and other Europeans—drawn to Hawaii's growing sugar and pineapple industries. Over time, the number of these new immigrants turned Hawaii's indigenous population into a minority. On Kauai, in fact, Filipinos now comprise 27% of the population, Japanese 26%, caucasians 22%, mixed-blood Hawaiians 18%, and pure-blooded, native Hawaiians only 2%.

In the late 1800s also, after the death of Kamehameha V, Hawaiian monarchy fell into disarray, and the custom of electing a king was established. At about this time, too, with the growth of Hawaii's sugar industry, American interests on the island increased. In 1892, upon the start of open rebellion, the *U.S.S. Boston* landed an armed force on the island of Oahu to protect American interests, and a year later, in 1893, a more or less bloodless revolution brought to power, at the head of a provisional government, Sanford B. Dole. The following year, Hawaii was declared a republic by the Hawaiian legislature, and on June 14, 1900, Hawaii was annexed, under the Organic Act, by the United States, and a territorial form of government established.

In 1902, Prince Jonah Kuhio Kalanianaole, born of royal parentage, and the last heir to the throne, became the first Hawaiian delegate elected to the U.S. Congress. Kuhio led the Hawaiian congressional delegation for the next two decades, and despite not having an official vote in the legislature—as Hawaii was only a territory of the United States at the time—he forged important legislation for the betterment of Hawaii and its people. Among his triumphs: the landmark Hawaiian Homesteads Act of 1910 and the Hawaiian Homes Commission Act of 1921, whereby public lands were made available to native Hawaiians for homesteading. He also obtained funding for such important projects as the Kahului Harbor, Maui's only deep-water port, and Pearl Harbor at Honolulu, and in 1919 and 1920, he introduced two successive bills for statehood for Hawaii in the U.S. Congress. In 1922, Kuhio died at the age of 50.

On August 21, 1959, Hawaii finally gained statehood, becoming the 50th state of the nation—the "Aloha State." That same year, the first commercial jet, a Boeing 707, landed in the islands, at Honolulu, greatly reducing travel time from the continental U.S. to Hawaii, to under 4½ hours. This, effectively, signalled the beginning of tourism in Hawaii.

In the following decade, Hawaii's tourist era began in earnest. On the island of Kauai, the Coco Palms Hotel, the island's first tourist hotel, which had originally been built as a 12-room hotel in 1953, expanded into a full-fledged, 390-room establishment in the 1960s. Also in the 1960s, Poipu Beach began to develop into a premier resort, beginning with the construction of the Waiohai Hotel—forerunner of the Waiohai Beach Resort—in the early 1960s and the Sheraton Kauai a few years later. In 1970, development began on the multimillion-dollar Princeville Resort, which included two golf courses, a shopping center and a small, commercial airport; and in the late 1970s the first Holiday Inn opened on Kauai's east side, near Wailua. During the 1980s, still more resort hotels sprang up on the island's south and east shores, including the Kauai Hilton, Kauai Beach Boy, Stouffer's and, grandest of all, the $350-million Westin Kauai.

In August, 1972, even as resort development continued unabated, the Palm Tree Ordinance was passed on Kauai, to minimize the impact of it all on the island and its inhabitants. The ordinance, effectively, restricted the height of all new buildings on the island to approximately that of a palm tree—40 feet, or four stories. The tallest building on the island now is the Westin Kauai, 10 stories high, originally built in 1959.

The 1950s, 60s, 70s and 80s also witnessed the creation of a series of state parks and sanctuaries, among them the Waimea Canyon and Koke'e state parks, originally established in 1952; Na Pali Coast State Park, encompassing 6,175 acres, established in 1962; Ha'ena State Park on Kauai's north shore and 917-acre Hanalei Valley Wildlife Refuge, established in 1972; and the Kilauea Point National Wildlife Refuge, with 160 acres set aside for endangered seabirds, established in 1988.

On November 23, 1982, Kauai suffered one of its worst setbacks, when Hurricane Iwa, with winds of nearly 95 miles per hour and waves breaking at heights of over 30 feet, devastated the island's south and west shores, destroying both resort and residential communities in the area, causing damage in excess of $200 million. And again, on September 11, 1992, Kauai bore the brunt of the single worst natural disaster in its history. Hurricane Iniki struck the island in all its fury, with sustained winds at 130 m.p.h. and gales up to 160 m.p.h. More than 7,000 homes on the island were razed and thousands left homeless; most hotels and resorts suffered severe damage, virtually all of the island's sugarcane and macadamia crop was lost, and Kauai's telephone, power and water systems failed. The hurricane left in its wake damage of nearly $2 billion.

Kauai has largely recovered since, and is now once again positioned as a premier destination resort, with an abundance of excellent hotel and condominium accommodations and restaurants and other visitor facilities, and a wealth of recreational opportunities, including swimming, surfing, snorkeling, scuba diving, waterskiing, kayaking, sailing, hiking, camping, golf, tennis, helicopter touring, and more.

◀❚ UP ❚ **1** ⑧⑧

1 = Area Segment

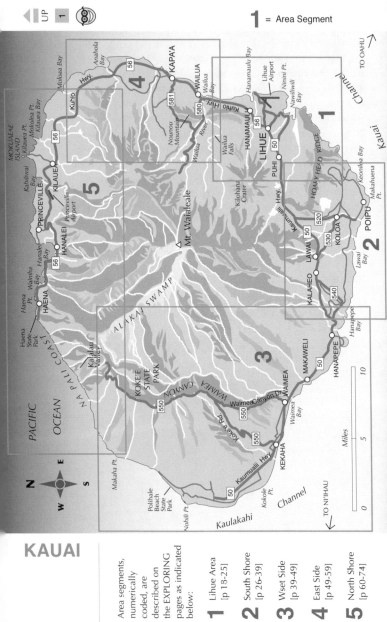

KAUAI

Area segments, numerically coded, are described on the EXPLORING pages as indicated below:

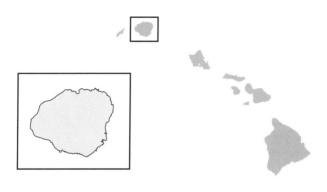

KAUAI | The Garden Isle

Kauai | Exploring the Island

Kauai is Hawaii's "Garden of Eden." It was the locale of *South Pacific, Jurassic Park, Raiders of the Lost Ark* and Elvis Presley's *Blue Hawaii*. It is *the* tropical paradise people dream about, with lush valleys and towering green mountains, cascading waterfalls and freshwater lagoons, secluded beaches and wild gardens bursting forth in bunches of plumeria, hibiscus, anthuriums, orchids, ginger and birds of paradise. Kauai is also Hawaii's oldest island, steeped in history and intertwined with Hawaii's mythical little people, the *menehune*, more than any other island.

Kauai encompasses approximately 558 square miles and is made up of a single volcanic land mass, largely centered around the 3,000-plus feet deep Wai'ale'ale crater (Mount Wai'ale'ale is also the highest point on the island, elevation 5,148 feet, and the wettest spot on earth, with an average annual rainfall of 451 inches). Like all the other Hawaiian islands, Kauai, too, has a dry, sunny side, the South Shore, and a rain-soaked, scenic one, the North Shore. In equally sharp contrast lie the island's East Side, home to Kauai's population centers of Lihue and Kapa'a, and its West Side, remote and sparsely populated.

For the purposes of exploring the island, we have divided Kauai into five logically-grouped, geographically-distinct sections:

1   **Lihue Area**, which includes Kauai's principal city, Lihue, and the area surrounding it;

2   **South Shore**, the area to the southwest of Lihue, along the island's south shore, which takes in Poipu, Koloa, Lawai and Kalaheo;

3   **West Side**, which includes Hanapepe, Waimea, Kekaha, Waimea Canyon and the Koke'e and Polihale state parks;

4   **East Side**, made up of the adjoining towns of Wailua and Kapa'a;

5   **North Shore**, which extends from Kilauea to Princeville, Hanalei and Ke'e Beach, and also includes the Na Pali Coast.

[The numbers in the sidebar correspond to those in the number-coded map of the island.]

LIHUE AREA | 1

Lihue | Kalapaki Beach | Kilohana | Wailua Falls

Lihue | 2 *See Map 2 on Page 19*

The best and most convenient place to begin your tour of Kauai, we might suggest, is Lihue, a small, urban center, situated on the southeast corner of the island, more or less equidistant from the east and north shores and the south and west shores—the two areas of visitor interest, which remain cut off from each other at the northwest end of the island by the rugged and largely inaccessible Na Pali Coast. Lihue is also the commercial and civic center of Kauai (and the nearby island of Ni'ihau), and home to Kauai's main airport, the Lihue Airport—which handles most of the island's commercial flights—as well as the island's principal port, Nawiliwili, situated just to the south of the center of town, where most of the cruise ships and freighters bound for Kauai anchor.

Rice Street | County Building, Bank of Hawaii Building, A.S. Wilcox Memorial Library Building, Kauai Museum

The Lihue township itself is rather uninspiring, but it does have a few places of visitor interest in and around it. Here, for instance, in the center of town, on Rice Street—the town's main street—you can search out a handful of 1930s buildings, most notably the old **3** **2** **County Building**, the **Bank of Hawaii Building** and the two-story **1** **A.S. Wilcox Memorial Library Building**. The last of these, the library building, now houses the **Kauai Museum**, which has several excellent exhibits centered around the history of Kauai—the oldest of the Hawaiian Islands—including scores of artifacts and old photographs and films depicting the "Story of Kauai," from the geological origins of the island to present day. There is also an art gallery on the premises, displaying works of local artists, and a gift shop with souvenirs and books of local interest.

Kalapaki Beach | Kalapaki Beach, Nawiliwili Bay, Kauai Marriott

Also, just to the south of the center of town, at the very bottom of Rice Street and Kapena Road, lies the sun-drenched, crescent-**9** shaped white-sand **Kalapaki Beach**. The beach is actually situated at ▶ the head of **Nawiliwili Bay**—Kauai's only deep-water harbor, built in the 1930s, and where, on any given day, you can see dozens of tug boats, fishing boats, sailboats and other pleasure craft, and,

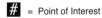

= Point of Interest

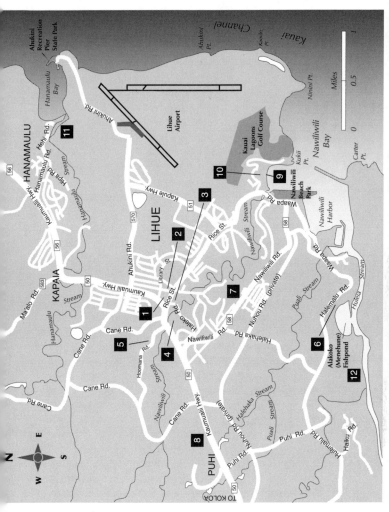

LIHUE
AREA

1. Kauai Museum
   (Wilcox Memorial
   Library Building)
2. County Building
3. Bank of Hawaii
   Building
4. Lihue Sugar Mill (1849)
5. Old Lutheran Church
   (1883)
6. Alakoko Fishpond
   Lookout
7. Grove Farm Homestead
8. Kilohana
9. Kalapaki Beach
10. Kauai Marriott
11. Hanamaulu Beach Park
12. Huleia National
    Wildlife Refuge

often enough, cruise ships, container ships and even U.S. naval vessels. Kalapaki Beach itself offers good swimming, surfing and sailing possibilities, and a little way from there, at the northeast corner of Nawiliwili Bay, you can visit Ninini Point, an excellent place for whale watching in season (December-April).

At Kalapaki Beach, too, at its west end, sits the landmark **Kauai** **10** **Marriott** resort hotel, a dazzling, $350-million extravaganza, originally built in 1987 by Chris Hemmeter, Hawaii's most famous resort developer, whose triumphs include the Westin Maui, Hyatt Regency Maui, Hyatt Regency Waikiki and the Hyatt Regency Waikoloa. The Kauai Marriott consists of five multi-storied buildings—3 to 10 stories high—with 356 luxury guest rooms, 4 restaurants, a mosaic-tiled, 26,000-square-foot swimming pool—one of the largest in Hawaii!—tennis courts, and two 18-hole, championship golf courses, the Kauai Lagoons Course and Kiele Course, both designed by Jack Nicklaus.

Around Lihue

Alakoko Fishpond Lookout, Grove Farm, Lihue Sugar Mill, Old Lutheran Church, Hanama'ulu Beach, Kilohana

6 Close at hand and also of interest is the **Alakoko Fishpond Lookout**, overlooking the ancient **Alakoko Fishpond** (also known as the Menehune Fishpond) and located on Hulemalu Road, just to the west of Nawiliwili Harbor. The lookout is reached by way of Rice Street south, and Nawiliwili Road (58) and Wilcox Road west and southwest, respectively, to Wa'apa Road, which, in turn, leads directly west to Hulemalu Road and so to the lookout. At any rate, the Alakoko Fishpond is said to have been built by Kauai's legendary little people, the *menehune*, who are believed to have carried the stones for the construction of the pond all the way from Makaweli, some 25 miles distant, passing them hand to hand along a double row of workers. The fishpond is located on the Hule'ia River—featured in the opening scenes of the *Indiana Jones* movie, *Raiders of the Lost Ark*—and has walls that are 5 feet high and 100 feet long, seen rising above the water. According to local lore, it was originally built at the request of a princess and her brother, who promised not to watch the *menehune* as they worked, but out of curiosity they did, and were subsequently turned to stone.

Also to be viewed from the lookout, lying adjacent to the **12** Menehune Fishpond, is the **Hule'ia National Wildlife Refuge**, a 241-acre wetlands preserve for endangered Hawaiian waterbirds. The refuge was originally established in 1973, and is now home to thirty-one species of birds, including the Koloa maoli (duck), moorhen, coot, and the Hawaiian stilt. However, in order to protect the endangered birds' habitat, the Hule'ia Refuge is closed to the public. Although some of the kayaking and other water tours often skirt the periphery of the preserve, offering visitors additional opportunities for viewing the refuge.

Another place of supreme interest, situated on Nawiliwili Road (58)—a mile or so southeastward from the intersection of Kaumuali'i Highway (50), or one and one-half miles northwest from Nawiliwili Harbor—is the **Grove Farm Homestead**, an authentic, 80-acre plantation-era estate. Grove Farm has some of the island's oldest plantation homes and buildings, nestled amid orchards, vegetable gardens and cattle pastures. The homestead was originally established by pioneer plantation owner George N. Wilcox in 1864, and has been wonderfully preserved in its original state, with period furnishings and fixtures and even some personal items, all of them more or less untouched—suspended in time—reflective of a bygone era. Guided tours are offered (by reservation only) of the build- ings—including the main plantation home and the cottages and workers' smaller camp houses—as well as the grounds.

Also of interest, a mile or so northwest from Grove Farm Home- stead on Nawiliwili Road (58) to the Kaumuali'i Highway (50), then eastward a little way on the Kaumuali'i Highway—just to the west of the intersection of Kaumuali'i and Kuhio highways—is the old **Lihue Sugar Mill**. The mill was originally built in 1849, when sugar was Kauai's principal industry and Lihue was at the center of that burgeoning industry. Interestingly, Lihue Sugar Mill is still in operation and now processes approximately 65,000 tons of sugar annually.

Nearby, too, just to the northwest of the sugar mill on Ho'omana Road—which goes off the Kaumuali'i Highway—stands the **Old Lutheran Church**, built in 1883 to service the large German popula- tion of the area at the time, and believed to be oldest Lutheran church in Hawaii.

North of Lihue, and also worth visiting, is **Hanama'ulu Beach Park**, situated at the head of Hanama'ulu Bay, and reached by way of Hanama'ulu Road east from the intersection of Kuhio Highway (56), roughly one third of a mile, then eastward another half mile on Hehi Road to the beach. Hanama'ulu Beach, bordered by ironwoods and quite popular with residents and visitors alike, has a good, safe swimming area, especially suited to children, as well as picnicking, fishing and camping possibilities.

There remains yet another place of interest, **Kilohana**, located on Kaumuali'i Highway (50), a little over a mile to the west of Lihue, and much to be recommended to first-time visitors to the area. Kilo- hana is the former plantation estate of Gaylord Wilcox—head of the Grove Farm Plantation during the 1930s and 1940s—situated on 35 acres amid sugarcane fields. The estate, largely restored—partly in the Art Deco style—now houses an interesting collection of shops and art galleries, the latter displaying works of prominent Hawai- ian artists, and a delightful courtyard restaurant, Gaylord's. There are also carriages here, drawn by Clydesdales, offering tours of the grounds as well as the nearby sugarcane fields.

A little to the west of Kilohana, on the *mauka*—inland— side of the highway (50), directly in front of the Kauai Community College, you can search out a Hawaiian Visitors Bureau marker depicting a Hawaiian warrior, which directs visitors' gazes to a natural rock formation on the slopes of the Hoary Head Mountains, known as
▶ **Queen Victoria's Profile**, with its likeness to the famous British monarch.

Wailua Falls

▶ A worthwhile detour from Lihue is the **Wailua Falls**, situated on the east side of Kauai, upriver from the Wailua township, but accessed from Lihue, northwestward on Ma'alo Road (583)—which goes off Kuhio Highway (56)—some 4 miles. The Wailua Falls are one of Kauai's premier visitor attractions, and the most photographed waterfalls on the island. The falls are actually twin waterfalls, located on the Wailua River, cascading some 80 feet. These are the very same falls that were featured in the opening scenes of the TV series *Fantasy Island*. Interestingly, in the early years the Wailua Falls were also the site of ceremonious leaps performed by the island's chiefs to prove their courage.

In any event, the waterfalls are reached by way of a short hike from the main road, Ma'alo Road, descending a half mile or so to a large, natural pool at the foot of the falls. There are also good picnicking possibilities here.

Accommodations | Lihue

Hotels

Marriott Kauai Resort and Beach Club. *$299-$665*. Kalapaki Beach, 3610 Rice St., Lihue; (808) 245-5050/(800) 220-2925/*www.marriotthawaii.com/kauai.html*. Rambling, luxury resort, with 345 rooms and 11 suites, situated on the beach. Facilities include an expansive swimming pool, health club and spa, tennis courts, two 18-hole golf courses, 2-acre tropical garden, walking and jogging trails and horse-drawn carriage and canopy-covered canoe tours of the resort and its lagoons and islands. Also restaurants and cocktail lounges, meeting rooms, and two shopping villages on premises.
Radisson Kauai Beach Resort. *$199-$459*. 4331 Kauai Beach Dr., Lihue; (808) 245-1955/(800) 333-3333/*www.radissonkauai*.

com. Beachfront hotel with 347 units with TV, phones and air conditioning. Swimming pool, tennis court, restaurant and cocktail lounge, meeting rooms, shops and beauty salon. Handicap facilities.

Tip Top Motel. *$49-$59*. 3173 Akahi St., Lihue; (808) 245-2333. 34 units, with TV, and air conditioning. Bakery, restaurant and cocktail lounge on premises.

Condominiums

Banyan Harbor Resort. *$120-$155*. 3411 Wilcox Rd., Lihue; (808) 245-7333/(800) 422-6926/*www.vacation-kauai.com*. 148 two-bedroom condominium units, located across the street from Kalapaki Beach. TV, phones, and full kitchen and laundry facilities. Swimming pool and tennis court on premises.

Castle Kaha Lani. *$175-$450*. 4460 Nehe Rd., Lihue; (808) 822-9331/(800) 367-5004/*www.castleresorts.com*. Oceanfront condominium complex with 65 one-, two- and three-bedroom units. TV, phones, full kitchens, laundry facilities. Also swimming pool, tennis courts and barbecue area.

Garden Island Inn. *$85-145*. 3445 Wilcox Rd., Lihue; (808) 245-7227/(800) 648-0154/*www.gardenislandinn.com*. 21 air-conditioned units with TV, refrigerators, microwave ovens, coffee makers, and ceiling fans. Daily maid service.

Kauai Beach Villas. *$119-$295*. 4330 Kauai Beach Dr., Lihue; (808) 241-1000/(888) 277-3701/*www.beachvillaskauai.com*. 150-unit condominium complex, located on the beach. Phones, TV, kitchenettes, and air conditioning. Swimming pool, tennis court.

Bed and Breakfast

Kauai Inn. *$79-$139*. 2430 Hulemalu Rd., Lihue; (808) 245-9000/(800) 808-2330/*wwwkauaiinn.com*. Historic, plantation-style inn with 48 units, situated on three acres. Phones, TV, microwaves, refrigerators. Some private balconies with ocean and mountain views; also pool on premises. Continental breakfast.

Dining | Lihue

[Restaurant prices—based on full course dinner, excluding drinks, tax and tips—are categorized as follows: *Deluxe*, over $30; *Expensive*, $20-$30; *Moderate*, $10-$20; *Inexpensive*, under $10.]

Barbecue Inn. *Inexpensive-Moderate.* 2982 Kress St., Lihue; (808) 245-2921. Popular local restaurant, serving Japanese and American food, including fresh fish, shrimp, steak, ribs, teriyaki pork, and sandwiches; also variety of pies. Open for lunch and dinner, Mon.-Sat.

Café Portofino. *Moderate-Expensive.* At the Marriott Kauai Beach Resort, 3610 Rice St., Suite 208, Nawiliwili; (808) 245-2121/*www.marriotthawaii.com.* Authentic Italian cuisine, featuring a variety of antipasto, homemade pasta, and such house specialties as eggplant parmigiana and scaloppini. Open-air dining, with panoramic views of Kalapaki Bay. Open for dinner. Reservations recommended.

Dani's Restaurant. *Inexpensive.* 4201 Rice St., Lihue; (808) 245-4991. Casual family restaurant, featuring Hawaiian, American and Japanese food, including lau lau, omelettes, steak, and teriyaki chicken, kalua pig and beef stew. Open for breakfast and lunch daily.

Duke's Canoe Club and Bar. *Moderate-Expensive.* At the Marriott Kauai Beach Resort, 3610 Rice St., Lihue; (808) 246-9599/245-5050/*www.hulapie.com/dukeskauai/index.html.* Exotic setting, overlooking Kalapaki Bay, and with a 30-foot waterfall splashing into a koi pond. Menu emphasizes island fare, including fresh fish and seafood, steak, prime rib, and salads. Good selection of appetizers. The establishment is named for legendary Hawaiian surfer Duke Kahanamoku, and houses a large collection of Duke memorabilia, including three of his surfboards. Open for lunch and dinner daily.

Garden Island. *Inexpensive.* 4252 Rice St., Lihue; (808) 245-8868. Informal restaurant. Extensive selection of authentic Chinese food. Open for lunch and dinner, Mon.-Sat.

Gaylord's at Kilohana. *Moderate.* At the historic Kilohana Plantation, 3-2087 Kaumuali'i Hwy., Puhi; (808) 245-9593/ *www.gaylordskauai.com.* American and Continental cuisine, including a variety of tropical specialties, served in a delightful courtyard setting in a 1935 plantation owner's home. Menu features fresh fish and island seafood and vegetables, venison, filet mignon, rack of lamb, prime rib, and pasta with grilled chicken. Desserts include homemade pies, parfaits, soufflés, cheesecakes and truffles. Open for lunch and dinner; also Sunday brunch. Reservations recommended.

Hamura's Saimin. *Inexpensive.* 2956 Kress St., Lihue; (808)

245-3271. Popular little restaurant, offering the quintessential "local experience." The favorite dish here is Saimen, a bowl of soup and noodles. Open for lunch and dinner.

Ho's Chinese Kitchen. *Inexpensive.* 3-2600 Kaumuali'i Hwy., Lihue; (808) 245-5255. Offers Mandarin and Szechuan dishes primarily. Open for lunch and dinner daily.

JJ's Broiler. *Inexpensive-Moderate.* At the Anchor Cove Shopping Center, 3416 Rice St., Nawiliwili; (808) 246-4422/(888) 246-4422/ *www.jjsbroiler.com.* Informal. open-air dining, with panoramic views of Kalapaki Bay. Traditional American fare, including home-made soups, sandwiches, salads, steak, seafood, pasta and chicken dishes, and freshly-baked bread rolls. Also cocktails. Open for lunch and dinner daily.

Kalapaki Beach Hut. *Inexpensive.* 3474 Rice St., Lihue; (808) 246-6330. Offers fresh island seafood and burgers and sandwiches. Informal setting. Open for breakfast, lunch and dinner daily.

Kauai Chop Suey. *Inexpensive-Moderate.* 3501 Rice St., Nawili-wili; (808) 245-8790. Popular family restaurant, famous for its chop suey. Also other Chinese favorites, such as won ton noodles and sweet and sour pork. Open for lunch and dinner, Tues.-Sun.

Kauai Lagoons Terrace Restaurant. *Moderate.* Kalapaki Beach, 3351 Ho'olauea Way, Lihue; (808) 241-6080. Open-air garden restaurant, offering lavish Pacific Rim buffets and island specialties; also salads, sandwiches and burgers. Cocktails. Open for breakfast and lunch daily.

Kukui's. *Expensive.* At the Marriott Kauai Beach Resort, Kalapaki Beach; (808) 246-5171/245-5050/(800) 220-2925/*www.marriot-thawaii.com.* Outdoor setting. International cuisine, including American and island specialties, and Pacific Rim buffets featuring prime rib and crab. Open for breakfast, lunch and dinner daily. Reservations suggested.

Naupaka Terrace Steak House. *Moderate-Expensive.* At the Radisson Kauai Beach Resort, 4331 Kauai Beach Dr., Lihue; (808) 246-5567/245-1955/(888) 805-3843/*www.radissonkauai.com.* Outdoor dining in exotic, torch-lit setting. Offers local seafood and midwestern aged beef; also prime rib and crab buffet, with salads, shrimp, roasted pork and all-you-can-eat crab. Open for breakfast, lunch and dinner daily. Reservations recommended.

Tip Top Cafe & Bakery. *Inexpensive-Moderate.* 3173 Akahi St., Lihue; (808) 245-2333. Centrally-located, family-style restaurant, serving primarily home-cooked American meals, and freshly baked breads and desserts, and their famous macadamia pancakes. Open for breakfast and lunch daily.

Whaler's Brew Pub. *Moderate-Expensive.* 3132 Ninini Point St., Lihue; (808) 245-2000. Pacific Rim cuisine, featuring fresh local seafood, steak, filet mignon, teriyaki chicken, oriental noodles and burgers, including a hallmark "Whale of a Burger.". Views of Kala-paki Bay. Open for lunch and dinner daily.

SOUTH SHORE | 2

Koloa | Poipu | Koloa Landing | Maha'ulepu | Lawai | Kalaheo

The South Shore of Kauai comprises, primarily, Poipu, the island's best known beach area, and the small towns of Koloa, Lawai and Kalaheo, as well as a series of beach parks dotted along the southern coast of the island—one of the driest and sunniest parts of Kauai.

| **Koloa** | *Tree Tunnel, Old Koloa Town, History Center, Koloa Church, St. Raphael's Church, Jodo Mission* | | *See Map 3 on Page 27* |

A good way to explore the South Shore of Kauai, we might suggest, is to go first to Koloa, reached by way of Kaumuali'i Highway (50), some 6 or 7 miles west from Lihue to the Koloa Gap—a natural pass between the Hoary Head Mountains to the south and the Wai'ale'ale range on the north—then Maluhia Road (520) south another 3 miles or so to Koloa. On Maluhia Road, just south of the intersection of the Kaumuali'i Highway, is the **Tree Tunnel**, one of the South Shore's most memorable and picturesque landmarks, where age-old swamp mahogany trees—a species of eucalyptus from Australia—line the road on either side, along a mile-long stretch, joining overhead to form a leafy tunnel. The eucalyptus trees were originally planted here in 1911—donated by local plantation owner Walter Duncan McBryde—to stabilize and reclaim swampland by utilizing the trees' root systems to absorb the excess water.

In any event, Koloa, meaning "long cane," is notable, first and foremost, as the birthplace of Hawaii's sugar industry, where William Hooper of Honolulu-based Ladd & Company arrived in 1835 and established a sugar plantation—the first in the islands. A **monument** located near the intersection of Maluhia and Koloa roads commemorates the event and honors the industry pioneers—both the first plantation owners and early field workers, the latter group comprised of Hawaiians, Chinese, Japanese, Portuguese, Koreans, Filipinos and Puerto Ricans. Adjacent to the monument, you can still see the remnants of the old stone chimney from the first sugar mill in Hawaii. Here you can also view the different strains of sugarcane found in the islands, and learn to distinguish between them.

Koloa itself is a small, quaint town, tourist oriented, and with an interesting little collection of shops, boutiques, art galleries and restaurants, most of them housed in old, plantation-era buildings in a section of town known as **Old Koloa Town**, that was largely restored in 1984. Here, too, housed in the historic, single-story **Koloa Hotel**, is the **Koloa History Center**, with several good exhibits and artifacts

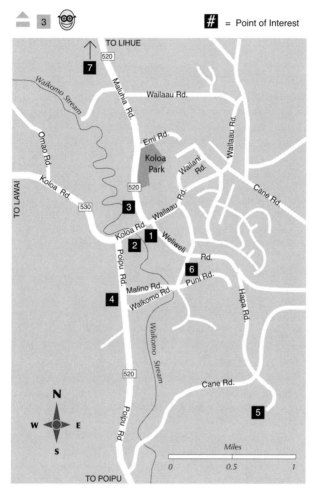

= Point of Interest

KOLOA

1. Old Koloa Town
2. Koloa History Center (Koloa Hotel)
3. Hawaii's First Sugar Mill
4. Koloa Church
5. St. Raphael's Church
6. Koloa Jodo Mission
7. Tree Tunnel

depicting the island's early-day sugar plantation era. The Koloa Hotel building itself dates from 1898, and is situated on the banks of the Waikomo Stream.

4 Nearby, just to the south on Poipu Road, is the picturesque, New England-style **Koloa Church**, originally established in 1835 by Reverend Peter Gulick, the first missionary assigned to Koloa; and to the southeast of there, at the bottom end of Hapa Road—which goes off Weliweli Road, which, in turn, goes off Koloa Road—

5 stands the historic **St. Raphael's Church**, the oldest Catholic church on Kauai, originally founded in 1841 and rebuilt in 1856 from coral and lava rock.

6 Also of interest here are two Japanese temples, **Koloa Jodo Mission** and **Koloa Hongwanji**, located at 3480 Waikomo Road and 5525 Koloa Road, respectively, both dating from 1910. The temples were originally built to serve the ethnic Japanese community during the early plantation days.

| **Poipu** | Sheraton, Kiahuna, Hyatt, Poipu Beach, Waiohai Beach, Shipwreck Beach, Brennecke's | | See Map 4 on Page 29 |

South of Koloa, some 2 miles or so on Poipu Road, lies Poipu, one of the island's best known beach resorts, centered around the popular Poipu Beach. Poipu Beach itself is a crescent-shaped, sandy, sun-drenched beach, and quite possibly among the best beaches in Hawaii, with excellent swimming, snorkeling, surfing and boogey-boarding possibilities. There are, besides, other beaches here as well—Sheraton, Shipwreck, Baby Beach, and Brennecke's—and a myriad hotels and condominiums, interspersed with several good restaurants and shops, and even a shopping center.

1 At any rate, at the west end of the Poipu Beach area—reached on Kapili Road, which goes off Poipu Road—stands the **Sheraton Kauai**, one of the first resort hotels developed at Poipu, originally built in the late 1960s. The hotel is situated on a 20-acre parcel that borders an especially lovely, palm-fringed beach, popularly known

13 as the **Sheraton Beach** (alternatively Poipu Beach or even Kiahuna Beach), which has good sunbathing, swimming, surfing and windsurfing possibilities. The hotel itself features 456 oceanview rooms in two separate wings, 2 stories and 4 stories high, respectively, as well as three restaurants, two swimming pools, children's wading pools, and tennis courts.

Close at hand also, a quarter mile or so east of the Sheraton Kauai on Poipu Road—on the *makai* (ocean) side of the road—are

5 the **Kiahuna Plantation Condominiums**, fronting on sunny **Poipu**

12 **Beach** (a.k.a. Sheraton Beach or Kiahuna Beach) and situated on the former estate of Hector and Alexandra Moir. The Moirs were

SOUTH SHORE | Poipu

UP 4 🎧

= Point of Interest

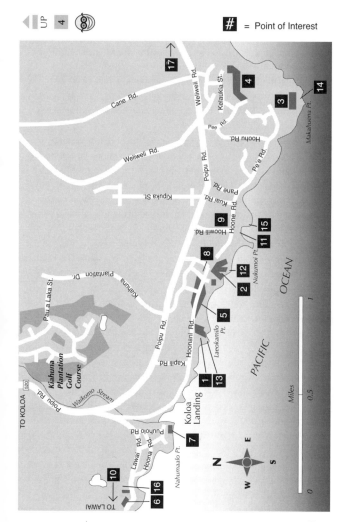

POIPU

1. Sheraton Kauai
2. Marriott Waiohai Beach Club
3. Hyatt Regency Kauai
4. Poipu Kai Resort
5. Kiahuna Plantation Condominiums
6. Lawai Beach Resort
7. Whaler's Cove Condominiums
8. Moir Gardens
9. Kilahuna Heiau
10. Spouting Horn
11. Poipu Beach Park
12. Poipu Beach
13. Sheraton Beach
14. Shipwreck Beach
15. Brennecke's Beach
16. Prince Kuhio Birthplace Monument
17. Maha'ulepu

avid gardeners who enthusiastically landscaped and planted their estate with a variety of tropical trees and plants. On the grounds of **8** Kiahuna Plantation you can still view the **Moir Gardens**, overflowing with plumeria, aloe, Hawaiian orchids, cacti and some 4,000 varieties of plants, and featured in the book, *Great Gardens of America*. Overlooking the gardens and of interest, too, is the Plantation Gardens Restaurant, which is actually housed in the 1930's former home of Mr. and Mrs. Moir.

2 Another place of interest at Poipu is the **Marriott Waiohai Beach Club**, consisting of eight four-story buildings, developed in 2004 and fronting on the crescent-shaped, sandy Poipu Beach. It is significant in that it is built on the site of the Waiohai Resort Hotel, which was seriously damaged during the 1992 hurricane Iniki, and which, in turn, was built on the site of the old Waiohai Hotel, Poipu's first hotel, developed in the early 1960s. Nearby, too, are the ruins of a 17th-century *heiau*, the Kilahuna Heiau, located di-**9** rectly across from the Waiohai, near a grove of palms. The **Kilahuna Heiau**, we must point out, was one of Kauai's most important *heiaus* once upon a time.

Yet another Poipu resort, farther east on Poipu Road, is the 600-**3** room **Hyatt Regency**, a luxury hotel, no less. It was originally built in 1991, at a cost of $220 million, amid a great deal of controversy over the hotel's selection of its building site—believed to be an ancient Hawaiian burial ground. In any case, the hotel has some good restaurants, swimming pools, tennis courts, and an 18-hole, Robert Trent Jones-designed golf course, sprawled over some 200 acres. **14** The hotel itself borders on **Shipwreck Beach**, a partly-sandy, partly-coral-lined beach, which offers excellent bodysurfing possibilities, although swimming is not encouraged here due to the strong ocean currents and sharp coral, making it rather unsafe for the activity.

Also of interest at Poipu, a little way to the east of the Marriott Waiohai Beach Club, at the foot of Ho'owili Road, which goes off **11** Poipu Road, is **Poipu Beach Park**, one of the south shore's most popular beach parks. Here you can visit Baby Beach, an especially good place for children to splash around, with a protective reef just off shore; and just to the east of there, another quarter mile or **15** so, lies **Brennecke's Beach**, a small pocket of sand, with excellent bodysurfing possibilities. Poipu Beach Park also has good public facilities, including pavilions, picnic tables, restrooms and showers.

Koloa Landing and Spouting Horn

Just west of Poipu on Ho'onani Road—which can also be accessed by way of Poipu Road south, Lawai Road southwest a little way, and so to Ho'onani Road—lies the historic **Koloa Landing**, an important port and center of commerce during the 1800s, when the town of Koloa, lying farther to the north, was at the heart of Hawaii's sugar industry. In fact, Koloa Landing, located at the mouth of Waikomo Stream, was once one of the largest ports in Hawaii, used by the Koloa Plantation to ship much of the island's sugar. It was also an important whaling port during the 19th century, second only to Lahaina and Honolulu, and for a brief period it even served as a port of entry, with a customs officer stationed there. In the early 1900s, however, with the ascendancy of nearby Port Allen and, later on, Nawiliwili as Kauai's principal ports, Koloa Landing was soon abandoned. The landing is now used primarily by scuba divers as a staging point.

Westward from Koloa Landing on Lawai Road, a mile or so, is **Prince Kuhio Park**, dedicated to Prince Jonah Kuhio Kalanianaole, where a monument marks the birthplace of the Hawaiian prince. Prince Kuhio was born in 1871 of royal parentage, and is well remembered as Hawaii's delegate to the United States Congress, where he served from 1903 to 1922. As a congressional delegate, Kuhio accomplished a great deal for the Hawaiian people, despite the fact that Hawaii was merely a territory of the United States at the time, rather than a state, and officially had no vote. One of his crowning accomplishments was the passage and implementation of the Hawaiian Homes Commission Act, whereby public lands have been made available to native Hawaiians for homesteading.

Close at hand, too, just west of Prince Kuhio Park, is **Lawai Beach**, a narrow, roadside beach that has good sunbathing, snorkeling, surfing and bodysurfing possibilities, with three surf breaks— "PK's," "Centers," and "Acid Drop"—all with consistently good waves, especially during the summer months.

Finally, another one and one-half miles westward from Lawai Beach on Lawai Road, and we are at Spouting Horn Beach Park, which has in it, as its chief attraction, **Spouting Horn**, one of Hawaii's most visited blowholes. Spouting Horn can be quite spectacular in action: a natural lava tube, through which steaming water gushes forth in a fountain at regular intervals, with the ebb and flow of the tide, as pressure builds from the sea swells. But before each gush of water comes a loud, roaring sound from the blowhole, of rushing air and water—but which, locals will tell you, are the moans of a legendary Hawaiian *mo'o* (lizard). The *mo'o*, we are told, was once returning from Ni'ihau to Kauai, after discovering his two sisters dead on the island of Ni'ihau; and in his mourning, blinded by his tears, he missed the landing and, instead, became trapped in the lava tube, where you can still hear him moaning.

Maha'ulepu

Gillin's Beach, Kawailoa Bay, Haula Beach

4   17 Another place of interest near the Koloa-Poipu area is **Maha'ulepu**, lying just to the east of Koloa—or northeast of Poipu—and reached by taking Poipu Road northeastward, passing by the Hyatt Regency, to the very end, then right—or southeast—onto a cane road that eventually leads to the coast at Maha'ulepu.

Maha'ulepu, which was once a densely populated area, but is now largely undeveloped, filled with sugarcane fields owned by the Grove Farm Company, encompasses a 2-mile stretch of coastline made up of three separate sections—Gillin's Beach, Kawailoa Bay and Haula Beach. The first of these, **Gillin's Beach**, can be reached by following the road leading to Maha'ulepu to the right—south-westward—at the three-way intersection at the very bottom. Gillin's Beach itself, named for a local manager of a plantation, is a narrow, sandy beach, quite popular with surfers and windsurfers. An added attraction here is a short walk north from Gillin's Beach, crossing over a stream and following it inland, which leads to a series of caves that are well worth investigating.

Next up, a half mile or so northeast from the three-way inter-section at the bottom of the road that leads to Maha'ulepu, lies Kawailoa Bay, a lovely, unspoiled coastal area backed by shallow sand dunes and groves of ironwood, with magnificent sea cliffs overhanging the bay at the eastern end and a sea stack rising from the ocean just off shore. Kawailoa Bay is frequented primarily by sunbathers, swimmers and fishermen, although, we must caution, the ocean currents along this coastal stretch can be quite danger-ous.

Finally, beyond Kawailoa Bay the road ends, and a little walk northeast along the shoreline from there brings us to **Haula Beach**, a surprisingly picturesque, secluded beach, backed by the 100-foot-high Aweoweo Sand Dunes. Haula Beach, however, offers only fair swimming conditions, primarily due to the coral and strong ocean currents.

Lawai and Kalaheo

McBryde Garden, Allerton Gardens, Kukuiolono Park

Lawai is a small, rural town that was once at the center of Kauai's pineapple industry, surrounded by fields of pineapple, but which now produces a variety of tropical fruit. The town lies approximately 10 miles west of Lihue on Kaumuali'i Highway (50), or 2 miles northwest of Koloa, reached from the latter on Koloa Road.

Lawai has two places of interest for the visitor: the National Tropical Botanical Garden's 252-acre McBryde Garden and the adjacent, 100-acre Allerton Garden, situated in the Lawai Valley at the southern end of Hailima Road, which goes southward off Koloa Road. The **National Tropical Botanical Garden** is of course one of the great botanical gems of Kauai, and the only nationally supported tropical garden, chartered by the United States Congress in 1964 and subsequently opened to public viewing in 1971. And its principal property here, the **McBryde Garden**, is a veritable treasure trove, with lavish displays of plants from tropical regions throughout the world. It is also notable as one of the world's big tropical research gardens, especially interesting to students of botany and serious gardeners. While the nearby **Allerton Gardens**, originally established in 1938 by Robert Allerton and his adopted son, John Gregg Allerton, feature, among other tropical plants, several rare South Pacific plants that were introduced to the island by the Allertons. At the gardens you can also visit the site of the home of Queen Emma, wife of King Kamehameha IV. The home stood here in its original state until 1992, when it was completely destroyed by the Hurricane Iniki; it was subsequently rebuilt. At any rate, both the McBryde and Allerton gardens can be toured by calling ahead for reservations, at (808) 742-2623.

Westward still, another 2 miles from Lawai (or 12 miles from Lihue) on Kaumuali'i Highway, lies Kalaheo—meaning "proud day"—another small town. Kalaheo is most notably the westernmost township on the island's south shore. Its chief interest lies in the **Kukuiolono Park**, located a mile or so south from the intersection of Kaumuali'i Highway (50) and Papalina Road, at the corner of Papalina and Pu'u roads. Kukuiolono Park has in it groves of eucalyptus, a delightful Japanese garden—quite popular for weddings, and also ideal for strolling around—and a small area devoted to Hawaiian exhibits, where you can view such artifacts as a stone bowl, a stone salt pan, and a stone lamp, among other artifacts. There is also a 9-hole public golf course at the park, with a clubhouse, overlooking the ocean.

Accommodations | Koloa, Poipu, Lawai, Kalaheo

Hotels

Embassy Vacation Resort. $385-$645. 1613 Pe'e Rd., Poipu; (808) 742-1888/(800) 349-4720/*www.kauaiembassy.com*. All-suite resort hotel, located on rocky bluff overlooking Shipwreck Beach, adjacent to the Hyatt Regency. 1- and 2-bedroom suites with microwave, refrigerator, safe, TV and phone. Private balconies or lanais. Jacuzzi and pool.

Hyatt Regency Kauai. *$365-$785.* 1571 Poipu Rd., Poipu; (808) 742-1234/(888) 591-1234/**(800) 554-9288**/*www.kauai.hyatt.com*. Luxury hotel, located on the beach. 600 rooms and suites, with TV, phones and air conditioning. Swimming pools, health club and spa, tennis courts and golf course. Shops, restaurants, cocktail lounges, and meeting rooms. Handicap facilities.

Sheraton Kauai Resort. *$325-$675.* 2440 Ho'onani Rd., Poipu; (808) 742-1661/(888) 847-0208/*www.sheraton-kauai.com*. Full-service oceanfront hotel, with 455 units. TV, phones, and air conditioning. Swimming pool, tennis courts, restaurants and cocktail lounge, meeting rooms, beauty salon. Handicapped facilities.

Condominiums and Cottages

Lawai Beach Resort. *$195-$405.* 5017 Lawai Rd., Poipu; (808) 742-9581/742-7400/(800) 367-8020/*www.suite-paradise.com*. 61 one- and two-bedroom condominium units with ocean views. TV, phones, kitchens, and daily maid service. Swimming pools, jacuzzis, tennis courts, gym. Handicap facilities.

Aston Poipu Kai Resort. *$185-$495.* 1775 Poipu Rd., Poipu; (808) 742-7424/(877) 997-6667/*www.aston-hotels.com*. 112 condominium units, with TV, phones, kitchens, and daily maid service. Adjacent to Brennecke's Beach and Shipwreck Beach. Swimming pools, tennis courts, restaurant and cocktail lounge on premises; also meeting room available.

Garden Isle Cottages. *$175-$190.* 2660 Pu'uholo Rd., Koloa; (808) 742-6717/(800) 742-6711/*www.oceancottages.com*. 9 oceanfront cottages, overlooking Koloa Landing. TV in cottages; swimming pool. Weekly maid service. Minimum stay, 2 days.

Outrigger Kiahuna Plantation. *$225-$470.* 2253 Poipu Rd., Poipu; (808) 742-6411/(800) 688-7444/*www.outrigger.com*. 197 condominium units, with TV, phones and kitchens. Swimming pool, tennis courts, restaurant and cocktail lounge. Daily maid service. Handicap facilities. Minimum stay, 2 days.

Koloa Landing Cottages. *$105-$185.* 2704B Ho'onani Rd., Koloa; (808) 742-1470/(800) 779-8773/*www.koloa-landing.com*. Studio units, and one- and two-bedroom self-contained cottages available for rental; TV and phones.

Makahuena at Poipu. *$180-450.* 1660 Pe'e Rd., Poipu; (808) 742-2482/(800) 367-5004/*www.castleresorts.com/MKH*. Ocean-front condominium complex with one-, two- and three-bedroom oceanfront, oceanview and garden-view units. TV, phones, refrigerator, microwave, laundry facilities; private lanais. Swimming pool, spa and tennis court on premises.

Nihi Kai Villas. *$135-$375.* 1870 Ho'one Rd., Poipu; (808) 742-1412/(800) 325-5701/*www.grantham-resorts.com/condos/nihikai. html*. 70 one-, two- and three-bedroom condominium units, most with ocean views, some with garden views. Located adjacent to Brennecke's Beach. TV, phones, laundry facilities. Swimming pool and tennis court.

Poipu Kapili. *$190-$550..* 2221 Kapili Rd., Koloa; (808) 742-6499/(800) 443-7714/*www.poipukapili.com*. 60 one- and two-bedroom condominium units, with TV, VCR and phones. Swimming pool, tennis courts.

Poipu Plantation. *$110-$190..* 1792-A Pe'e Rd., Poipu; (808) 742-6757/(800) 634-0263/*www.poipubeach.com*. 9 units in condominium complex, with ocean and garden views, located within easy distance of Poipu Beach. TV, phones, ceiling fans, and kitchens; library and laundry for guests' use. Also, bed and breakfast inn on site (see below); rates from $95.00.

Poipu Shores. *$200-$550.* 1755 Pe'e Rd., Koloa; (808) 742-7700/(800) 367-5004/*www.castleresorts.com/PSC*. 33 oceanfront condominiums units, with one, two and three bedrooms. TV, phones, full kitchens; swimming pool and barbecue area.

Prince Kuhio Resort. *$115-150.* 5061 Lawai Rd., Koloa; (808) **745-8841**/(800) 367-5025/*www.princekuhiokauai.com or www. kauai-vacation.com*. 48 condominium units, close to beach. TV, kitchen facilities, swimming pool.

Waikomo Stream Villas. *$99-$175.* 2721 Poipu Rd., Poipu; (808) 742-7220/(800) 325-5701/*www.grantham-resorts.com/condos/ waikomo.html*. 33 one- and two-bedroom condominium units with TV, phones, and kitchens. Swimming pool and tennis court. Maid service available upon request. Minimum stay, 3 days.

Whalers Cove. *$349-$639.* 2640 Pu'uholo Rd., Koloa; (808) 742-7571/(800) 367-7052/(800) 225-2683/*www.whalers-cove.com*. 38 oceanfront condominium units with garden and ocean views. TV, phones, ceiling fans and kitchen. Daily maid service. Minimum stay is 2 nights.

SOUTH SHORE | Accommodations

Bed and Breakfast

Bamboo Jungle House. $110. 3829 Waha Rd., Kalaheo, HI 96741; (808) 332-5515/(888) 332-5115/*www.kauai-bedandbreakfast.com*. Plantation-era home with 3 guest rooms with tropical furnishings. Tropical garden setting, with exotic plants and flowers, and waterfalls splashing into pool. Also hot tub and jacuzzi. Full breakfast with an entree, freshly-baked breads, fresh island fruit and local Kauai coffee.

Classic Vacation Cottages. *$50-$150. P.O. Box 901,* 2687 Onu Place, Kalaheo, HI 96741; (808) 332-9201/*www.classiccottages. com*. 4 self-contained cottages, with TV and kitchens, situated in rural, country surroundings, not far from the South Shore beaches. Daily maid service. Continental breakfast available for an additional charge of around $5.00. Minimum stay, 2 days.

Gloria's Spouting Horn Bed & Breakfast. *$325-$400.* 4464 Lawai Rd., Koloa, HI 96756; (808) 742-6995/*www.gloriasbedandbreakfast.com*. Tropical beach house. 3 guest rooms with private baths; also ceiling fans, refrigerators, and TV in rooms. Pool. Extended tropical breakfast. Minimum stay, 2 days. Also available are three small self-contained cottages, each with 1 bed, 1 bath, full kitchen. Rates range from $150-$225.

Hale Ikena Nui. $70-$100. 3957 Uluali'i St., Kalaheo, HI 96741; (808) 332-9005/(800) 332-0911/550-0778/*www.kauaivacationhome.com*. One-bedroom suite in South Shore oceanview home. Fully-equipped kitchen, TV, phone, barbecue grill and lanai. Private entrance. Full breakfast.

Marjorie's Kauai Inn. *$110-$130.* P.O. Box 866, 3307-D Hailima Rd., Lawai, HI 96765; (808) 332-8838/(800) 717-8838/**443-9180**/*www.marjorieskauaiinn.com*. Situated on 1-acre property with views of Lawai Valley. Offers 3 guest rooms with private baths and lanais; also in-room TV and phone, microwave and refrigerator. Outdoor hot tub and spa, in gazebo.

Poipu Bed & Breakfast and Kauai Inn. *$125-$150.* 2720 Ho'onani Rd., Poipu; (808) 742-1146/245-9000/(800) 808-2330/ *www.kauaiinn.com*. Restored, 1933 plantation home, located one block from the beach. 7 rooms with private baths; TV, refrigerators, ceiling fans. Tropical continental breakfast and afternoon tea.

Poipu Bed and Breakfast. *$95-$110.* At the Poipu Plantation Resort, 1792-A Pe'e Rd., Koloa, HI 96756; (808) 742-6757/(800) 634-0263/*www.poipubeach.com*. 4 classic rooms and suites—including a honeymoon suite—in 1938 plantation-era house. Island decor with tropical furnishings; TV, ceiling fans, private baths. Garden views. Also lanai room and cozy parlor. Fresh, hearty breakfast.

South Shore Vista. *$64-$79.* 4400 Kai Ikena Dr., Kalaheo, HI 96741; (808) 332-9339/(888) 332-9339/*www.southshorevista. com*. One-bedroom apartment in South Shore home. Kitchen, bath with full tub, cable TV, private lanai. Ocean and mountain views. . Breakfast with fresh fruit and hot cereal. Minimum stay, 3 nights.

Dining | Koloa, Poipu, Lawai, Kalaheo

[Restaurant prices—based on full course dinner, excluding drinks, tax and tips—are categorized as follows: *Deluxe*, over $30; *Expensive*, $20-$30; *Moderate*, $10-$20; *Inexpensive*, under $10.]

Armoré Ristoranté. *Expensive-Deluxe.* At the Sheraton Kauai, 2440 Ho'onani Rd., Poipu; (808) 742-1661/*www.sheratonkauai. com*.Traditional Italian cuisine, served in oceanfront setting. Menu features a good selection of pasta dishes, including lasagna and lobster ravioli; also pork and veal preparations, and salads. Open for dinner daily. Reservations recommended.

Brennecke's Beach Broiler. *Moderate.* 2100 Ho'one Rd., Poipu; (808) 742-7588/(888) 384-8810/*www.brenneckes.com*. Beachfront restaurant in outdoor setting, overlooking Poipu Beach. House specialties include kiawe char-broiled fresh island fish, steak, and lobster tail. Also on the menu are chicken and pasta dishes, barbecued ribs and sandwiches. Located directly across from Poipu Beach Park. Lunch and dinner daily. Reservations suggested.

Brick Oven Pizza. *Inexpensive-Moderate.* 2-2555 Kaumuali'i Hwy., Kalaheo; (808) 332-8561. Family-style pizzeria, featuring a variety of pizzas, including vegetarian pizzas, and homemade sausages and salads. Open for lunch and dinner daily (except Mondays).

Café Di Amici. *Moderate-Expensive.* 2301 Nalo Rd., Poipu; (808) 742-1555. Italian restaurant, serving traditional Italian food with local flavor, including a variety of pasta dishes with prawns, lobster, smoked salmon and chicken, served with an assortment of homemade sauces; also veal piccata, scampi and saltimbocca. Good selection of Italian wines. Open for dinner daily. Reservations suggested.

Camp House Grill. *Inexpensive-Moderate.* Cnr. Kaumuali'i Hwy. (50) and Papalina Rd., Kalaheo; (808) 332-9755. Housed in wooden, tin-roofed structure, reminiscent of the plantation days. Offers primarily hamburgers, barbecued chicken and island fish, and freshly-baked, homemade pies. Open for breakfast, lunch and dinner.

Dondero's. *Deluxe.* At the Hyatt Regency Kauai, 1571 Poipu Rd., Poipu; (808) 240-6456/742-1234, ext. 4900/*www.kauai.hyatt. com*. Elegant Northern Italian restaurant, overlooking Shipwreck Beach. Specialties include fresh pasta with grilled chicken breast, veal, filet, rack of lamb, lobster and Pacific Northwest salmon; also classic salads and traditional Italian soups. Extensive wine list. Live

SOUTH SHORE | Dining

entertainment. Open for dinner. Reservations required.

Poipu Beach Broiler. *Moderate.* At the Poipu Kai Resort, 1941 Poipu Rd., Poipu; (808) 742-6433. Casual eatery in spacious dining room. Menu features fresh island fish, seafood, prime rib and sirloin; also salads, sandwiches and burgers on lunch menu. Open for lunch and dinner daily.

Ilima Terrace. *Moderate.* At the Hyatt Regency Kauai, 1571 Poipu Rd., Poipu; (808) 742-1234, ext. 4242/*www.kauai.hyatt.com.* Open-air dining in tropical garden setting, with waterfalls and koi ponds; overlooking Shipwreck Beach. Buffet-style dining with buffet themes changing daily; also salads and sandwiches for lunch. Buffet breakfast features tropical fruit; lavish champagne brunch on Sundays. Open for breakfast, lunch and dinner daily, and brunch on Sundays. Reservations suggested.

Kalaheo Steak House. *Inexpensive-Moderate.* 4444 Papalina Rd., Kalaheo; (808) 332-9780. American fare, served in rustic dining room with hardwood tables. House specialties are teriyaki pork tenderloin and shrimp scampi; also steaks, chicken and fresh seafood. Dinner daily.

Keoki's Paradise. *Moderate-Expensive.* In the Poipu Shopping Village, Poipu; (808) 742-7534. Tropical, Polynesian setting, amid pools and lush greenery. Favorites here are fresh Hawaiian fish, lobster, steak, prime rib and ginger chicken. Open for dinner. Reservations suggested.

Naniwa. *Expensive.* At the Sheraton Kauai, 2440 Ho'onani Rd., Poipu; (808) 742-1661/*www.sheratonkauai.com.*. Oceanfront Japanese restaurant. Features sushi bar and traditional Japanese menu items, including tempura, sashimi, and miso soup. Japanese buffet on Saturdays. Open for dinner, Tues.-Sat. Reservations recommended.

Pattaya Asian Café. *Moderate.* 2360 Kiahuna Plantation Dr., Poipu; (808) 742-8818. Pleasant outdoor café, serving primarily Thai cuisine, with a good selection of curries. Open for lunch and dinner daily.

Plantation Gardens Restaurant. *Moderate-Expensive.* At the Kiahuna Plantation Resort, 2253 Poipu Rd., Poipu; (808) 742-2216. Housed in historic plantation house in tropical setting, amid lush gardens. Offers Pacific Rim cuisine, featuring crab-stuffed fish, mahi mahi macadamia, and Pacific lobster. Cocktails. Open for dinner. Reservations suggested.

Roy's Poipu Bar & Grill. *Moderate-Expensive.* In the Poipu Shopping Village, 2360 Kiahuna Plantation Dr., Poipu; (808) 742-5000/*www.roysrestaurant.com.* "Hawaiian Fusion Cuisine," blending local island ingredients with Asian spices and garnishes and European-flavor sauces. Menu features blackened island ahi, hibachi-style grilled salmon, mahi mahi, ribs, potstickers and shrimp. Also hot chocolate souffle. Open for dinner daily. Reservations recommended

Shells Restaurant. *Moderate-Expensive*. At the Sheraton Kauai, 2440 Ho'onani Rd., Poipu; (808) 742-1661/*www.sheratonkauai. com*. Outdoor terrace restaurant, overlooking beach. Features island buffets, and fresh fish, seafood, steak, lamb, and pasta dishes. Also seafood buffet on Fridays. Open for breakfast and dinner daily. Reservations recommended.

Taqueria Nortenos. *Inexpensive*. 2827 Poipu Rd., Poipu; (808) 742-7222. Casual Mexican restaurant, with Spanish decor. Offers Sonoran food—tacos, burritos, tostadas, and freshly-prepared enchiladas and chile rice. Take-outs available. Lunch and dinner daily.

Tidepools. *Expensive-Deluxe*. At the Hyatt Regency Kauai, 1571 Poipu Rd., Poipu; (808) 742-1234/. Well-regarded restaurant, housed in thatched Polynesian huts surrounded by lagoons, with ocean views. Menu features fresh, broiled fish, and steak, lobster and prime rib; also some vegetarian dishes. Cocktails. Dinners daily. Reservations recommended.

WEST SIDE | 3

Hanapepe | Waimea | Kekaha | Waimea Canyon | Koke'e State Park

The West Side of Kauai describes, quite broadly, the west shore of the island, characteristically wild and remote. It includes the towns of Hanapepe, the most important, and Waimea and Kekaha, and also takes in, for the purposes of touring, the spectacular Waimea Canyon and Koke'e State Park, both of which lie farther inland from the coast.

Hanapepe | *Lookout, Port Allen, Salt Pond, Russian Fort* | 5 | *See Map 5 on Page 41*

The principal town on the west side of the island is of course Hanapepe, lying approximately 4 miles west of Kalaheo, or 16 miles from Lihue, and reached more or less directly on Kaumuali'i Highway (50). But first, before Hanapepe, some 2 miles west of Kalaheo and located alongside the highway, is the **Hanapepe Valley** **Lookout** which offers sweeping views of the lush Hanapepe Valley as it fans out toward the center of the island. And two miles farther, southwestward from the lookout on the highway, lies the little town of Ele'ele, with a handful of shops and, notably, **Port Allen**, a small boat harbor that can be reached on Waialo Road (Highway 541)—which goes south off Kaumuali'i Highway (50). During the late 1800s and early 1900s, before the development of Nawiliwili Harbor at Lihue in the 1930s, Port Allen was Kauai's main port.

In any case, Hanapepe is "Kauai's Biggest Little Town" and the West Side's largest and most important community. It is situated in the heart of an agriculturally rich region that supplies the island with much of its produce. It is also, we might add, notable as the Bougainvillea Capital of Hawaii, abundant in the colorful flowers, with hills covered with bougainvilleas rolling back from the highway on the approaches to Hanapepe. The town itself lies at the head of Hanapepe Bay, and is filled with shops, restaurants and art galleries. It is also recognizable from its main street, Hanapepe Road, which provided the setting for the television mini-series, *The Thorn Birds*.

Just to the south of Hanapepe, and also of interest, is the **Salt Pond Beach Park**, reached by way of Lele Road south off the highway (50), just past mile marker 17, then right onto Lokokai Road, to the very end. Here, on the *makai*—ocean—side of Lokokai Road, you can see some ancient salt ponds, used by Hawaiians for hundreds of years, to make salt. Typically, sea water is pumped into the ponds and left to evaporate in the sun, leaving only the crystallized salt in the mud-lined beds, which is then drained further, and bagged and made ready for market. At the Salt Pond Beach Park there are some pavilions, picnic tables, restrooms and showers and restroom facilities, and the beach here has good swimming possibilities to boot, with a protective reef just offshore.

Westward from Hanapepe lie the small plantation towns of Kaumakani, Olokele and Pakala, where sugar is still the principal industry. There is little to interest the visitor in these towns, however, save for a surf break at Pakala, known as "Pakalas" or "Infinities," with its exceptionally long waves that are especially spectacular during the summer months. There are also good views of Ni'ihau from here, looking southwestward, directly across the Kaulakahi Channel. The beach can be reached by way of a dirt trail that dashes off through a sugarcane field, *makai* from the highway (50), at mile marker 21, to the ocean, then east a little way to the beach.

Farther still, another one and one-half miles west from Pakala —some 22 miles west of Lihue—lies the **Russian Fort Elizabeth State Park**, a 17-acre park, situated largely on the east bank of the Waimea River. Here you can still see the ruins of the Russian fort—for which the park is named—dating from 1817. The fort was originally built for the Russians by a German architect, Georg Anton Scheffer, and named for Czarina Elizabeth, wife of Alexander I. In 1817, however, not long after its construction, the fort was abandoned by the Russians and subsequently occupied by Hawaiians until 1864, when it was finally closed. A self-guided walk leads past remnants of a fort wall—with its star-like projections, where canons were once placed—and through the fort, where you can still see the layout of the quarters, armory and barracks.

WEST SIDE | Hanapepe

 # = Point of Interest

UP 5

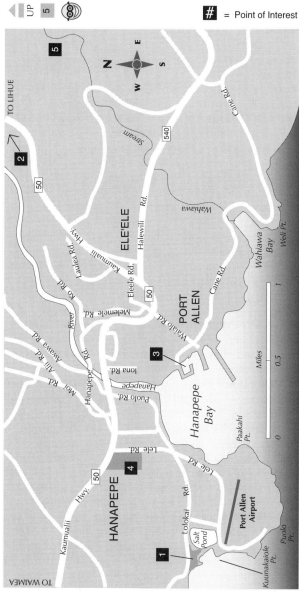

TO LIHUE

50

2

540

Stream

Cane Rd.

5

N
E
W
S

ELE'ELE

Halewili Rd.

Wahiawa

Kaumualii Hwy.

Laulea Rd.

Ko Rd.

Eleele Rd.

50

Melemele Rd.

River Rd.

PORT
ALLEN

Waialo Rd.

Cane Rd.

Wahiawa
Bay

Well Pt.

Mor. Rd.

Alili Rd.

Awawa Rd.

Hanapepe Rd.

Iona Rd.

Puolo Rd.

Hanapepe

3

Hanapepe
Bay

Paakahi
Pt.

Miles

0.5

1

0

HANAPEPE

Lele Rd.

4

50

Kaumualii Hwy.

Lolokai Rd.

Lele Rd.

Salt
Pond

1

Port Allen
Airport

Puolo
Pt.

Kuunakaiole Pt.

TO WAIMEA

HANAPEPE

1. Salt Pond
   Beach Park
2. Hanapepe
   Valley
   Lookout
3. Small Boat
   Harbor
4. Hanapepe
   Park
5. Petroglyphs

WEST SIDE | Waimea

Waimea

*Waimea Foreign Church,
Hawaiian Church,
Menehune Ditch*

See Map 6
on Page 43

The next major town, a half mile or so northwestward from Fort Elizabeth State Park on Kaumuali'i Highway, just over the Waimea River, is Waimea, with its associations to Captain James Cook. In fact, Waimea is the site of Cook's first landing in Hawaii, on January 20, 1778. A **statue** of Captain Cook is located in the center of town, on the highway itself, and a **plaque**, also commemorating his landing, is placed at **Lucy Wright Beach Park**—at the actual site of the landing on the west bank of the Waimea River—which lies on the *makai*—ocean—side of the highway as you enter the town of Waimea. The park has some public facilities, including showers and restrooms, as well as camping possibilities and a beach with driftwood.

Waimea is also notable as the first place on the island to host western missionaries. In fact, it has in it one of the island's most distinctive missionary-era churches: the **Waimea Foreign Church**, a New England-style church, dating from 1859 and constructed from stone blocks, which was 12 years in the making. The church is situated at the corner of Tsuchiya and Makeke roads. Another church, the **Waimea Hawaiian Church**, originally built in 1872, stood on Kaumuali'i Highway (50), near the corner of Hale Road, until it was completely destroyed in 1992 by the hurricane Iniki. However, the site of the church can be visited.

Another place of interest here, located just to the north of the Waimea township—some 1½ miles on Menehune Road which heads out from the center of town, off Kaumuali'i Highway—is the ancient **Menehune Ditch**. The ditch is a feat of engineering, no less, and the handiwork of Kauai's legendary and industrious little people, the *menehune*. The *menehune*, we are told, were a mysterious people who worked only at night and completed entire projects in the course of a single night. Their ingenuity, dexterity and knowledge of construction can be witnessed in some of the early-day architectural examples in the islands that have been attributed to them, with the characteristic flanged and fitted cut-stone bricks interlocking in a manner that is unique to the *menehune*. The Menehune Ditch—or what is left of it—is perhaps the most famous work of these pixie-like ancient people. The ditch was originally built as an aqueduct, some 24 feet high, to irrigate the *taro* patches in the valley. Today, only a small portion of the ditch is visible, although it remains a marvel of no small measure.

WEST SIDE | Waimea

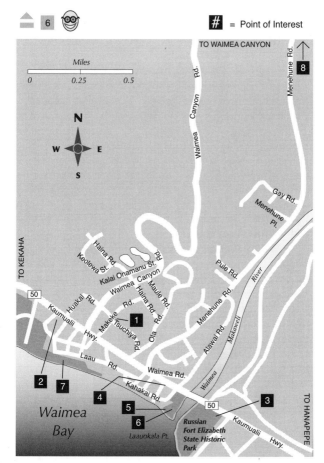

= Point of Interest

TO WAIMEA CANYON

WAIMEA

1. Waimea Foreign Church
2. Site of Waimea Hawaiian Church
3. Russian Fort
4. Captain Cook Statue
5. Captain Cook Landing Place
6. Lucy Wright Beach Park
7. Waimea Recreational Pier State Park
8. Menehune Ditch

Kekaha

Kekaha Sugar Mill, Polihale State Park, Queen's Pond

Kekaha is the next town along, some 3 miles west of Waimea on Kaumuali'i Highway. It is essentially a sugar plantation town which has at its center the **Kekaha Sugar Mill**, and where sugar is still the principal industry.

Also at Kekaha is the Kekaha Beach Park, situated near the northwest end of town. The park, most importantly, marks the beginning of a pristine, secluded—even desolate—white-sand beach that stretches some 12 miles along the largely uninhabited western end of the island, to Polihale State Park, which lies farther to the north. Kekaha Beach is frequented mostly by surfers and fishermen, with swimming not advised here, primarily due to the strong rip tides and longshore ocean currents.

Approximately midway between Kekaha Beach Park and Polihale State Park, off the highway (50), is the Pacific Missile Range Facility, an area used for underwater missile testing and rocket launches, owned and operated by the U.S. Navy. Here, too, is Majors Bay, a popular beach, and one of the best places on the west side for surfing, accessed through the naval base. And again, swimming is not encouraged here due to the unsafe ocean conditions.

Finally, at **Polihale State Park** the road ends. Polihale—also known as "Barking Sands" due to the crunching sound of the sand underfoot—is one of the most beautiful beaches in the Hawaiian islands, some 4 miles long and almost a hundred yards wide on the average. It is backed by 50- to 100-foot-high sand dunes and overhung, at its northern end, by lofty sea cliffs that are situated at the beginning—or southwestern end—of the fabulous Na Pali Coast. Polihale State Park is reached by way of Kaumuali'i Highway a mile or so past the Pacific Missile Range Facility, then left—toward the coast—another 3½ miles on a sign-posted, bumpy dirt road, passing through fields of sugarcane, to a large monkey pod tree at a fork in the road; at the fork, go right—or north—a little over one and one-half miles, directly to the Polihale State Park day use area. There are some pavilions with picnic tables at the day use area, as well as showers and restrooms facilities. But once again, be forewarned that the ocean conditions here are unsafe for swimming, with strong, unpredictable currents.

Also in the Polihale area is a coastal strip known as **Queen's Pond**, named for a Kauaian queen who once bathed here, and reached on the same Polihale dirt road—which goes off the highway (50)—to the monkey pod tree at the fork, then left—or south—a little way to Queen's Pond. Surprisingly, there is a safe swimming area here, protected by a reef just offshore, although high surf waves are known to frequently crash over the reef, creating unusually strong currents, especially during the winter months.

Waimea Canyon

  7

*See Map 7
on Page 46*

There are two routes leading into Waimea Canyon, located on the west side of the island, more or less directly north of Waimea. The first of these, Koke'e Road, heads out from Kekaha northeastward, offering views of the ocean and the Kekaha township; while the other, quite possibly the more popular of the two and also more scenic, the Waimea Canyon Drive, goes directly north from Waimea, some 6 miles *mauka*—inland—to intersect Koke'e Road, then onward through Waimea Canyon to finally emerge at Koke'e State Park. Also on Waimea Canyon Drive, some 4 miles from the intersection of Kaumuali'i Highway, is a roadside **lookout** at an elevation of 1,000 feet, with commanding views of the canyon and, to the south, the town of Waimea and the Pacific Ocean. Worth stopping at, too, is the **Kukui Trailhead**, situated at an elevation of 3,000 feet, from where the Iliau Nature Trail journeys around a half-mile loop, rewarding hikers with panoramic views of the canyon. Another, the Kukui Trail, also heads out from the Kukui Trailhead, leading hikers along a strenuous, 2½-mile trek, descending some 2,500 feet to the Waimea River.

In any event, Waimea Canyon is famous as the "Grand Canyon of the Pacific"—a 2,850-foot-deep canyon, 10 miles long and 2 miles wide, carved, over time, by rivers, streams and the weather. It is really quite spectacular with its maze of gullies and spires, bathed in rich hues of red, brown and green, continually changing with the light. There are also three lookouts here—the Waimea Canyon Lookout, Pu'u ka Pele Overlook, and the Pu'u Hinahina Viewpoint—all offering different perspectives on the canyon. The **Waimea Canyon Lookout**, for one, at an elevation of 3,400 feet, offers superb views of the canyon walls and various streams emerging from the center of the island at Wai'ale'ale. Some 3 miles farther, at the **Pu'u ka Pele Overlook**, you can see the Waipo'o Falls cascading some 800 feet—only if there has been some rain, though. And another mile from the Pu'u ka Pele Overlook is the **Pu'u Hinahina Viewpoint**, where there are actually two lookouts, one with views of the island and the town of Hanapepe, and the other overlooking the nearby island of Ni'ihau.

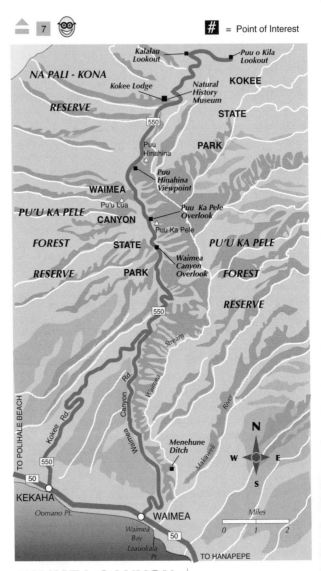

= Point of Interest

WAIMEA CANYON

Koke'e State Park

Koke'e Lodge, History Museum, Kalalau Lookout 7 *See Map 7 on Page 46*

Northward from Waimea Canyon lies Koke'e State Park, situated at an elevation of 3,600 feet, and with temperatures that are typically 10°-15° cooler than at sea level. The park encompasses more than 4,600 acres and boasts several miles of hiking trails, scores of picturesque waterfalls, and scenic vistas throughout. Also at the park, some 2 miles north of the Pu'u Hinahina Viewpoint on Koke'e Road, are the **Koke'e Lodge**—which serves breakfast, lunch and dinner, and offers rental cabins for overnight stays—and the adjacent **Natural History Museum**. The museum has a good display of Hawaiian artifacts and information on the area's wildlife, as well as an excellent book section devoted to Hawaiiana, where you can also find maps—including trail maps—for the area. Additionally, at the museum you can obtain current information on the area's trails, including an update on trail conditions.

However, among the most popular pursuits at Koke'e State Park is hiking, with a variety of trails—for all levels of fitness and training—and well-marked trailheads throughout the park. Here, for instance, on Koke'e Road itself, on either side of mile marker 17, are the Awa'awa'puhi and Kaluapuhi trailheads, with trails leading down into the valley; and 2 miles farther, more or less at the end of Koke'e Road, are trailheads for trails leading into the Alakai Swamp, which lies just below Mount Wai'ale'ale. Mount Wai'ale'ale is of course the highest point on the island, at an elevation of 5,148 feet, and is notable, too, as the wettest spot on earth, with an average annual rainfall of 451 inches! It is also responsible for feeding many of the streams on Kauai, filtering much of the rain water here into the scores of tributaries and rivers. At any rate, hiking through the Alakai Swamp can be challenging, yet rewarding, with trails winding through native rain forests and bogs, where you could quite conceivably find yourself knee-deep in mud.

Also at Koke'e State Park are the **Kalalau Lookout** and the **Pu'u o Kila Lookout**, located at mile marker 18 and at the end of Koke'e Road, respectively. Both lookouts offer good views of the Kalalau Valley, where an ancient Hawaiian settlement once flourished, with little or no contact with the outside world, until the growing urban centers of the island lured the last of the inhabitants from this lush valley. The Kalalau Lookout, by the way, at an elevation of 4,000 feet, also overlooks the stunning Na Pali Coast to the north.

WEST SIDE | Accommodations / Dining

Accommodations | Waimea, Kekaha, Koke'e

Koke'e Lodge. *$59-$69.* Located in the Koke'e State Park, on Koke'e Rd., 13 miles north of Waimea; (808) 335-6061/*www.kokee-kauai.com*. 12 cabins with kitchens. Restaurant and cocktail lounge, and shops nearby. Minimum stay, 2 days; maximum stay, 5 days.

Kauai Harbor House. *$368-$399.* 8949 Kaumuali'i Hwy., #50, Kekaha; (808) 338-1625/(800) 992-4632/*www.kauai-harborhouse.com* or *www.aston-hotels.com*. 3-bedroom, 3-bath, newly-refurbished harbor house, nestled on 2-acre oceanfront estate. Nearby Waimea Plantation Cottages facilities available to Kauai Harbor House guests, including swimming pool and tennis and volleyball courts.

Waimea Plantation Cottages. *$140-$735.* 9400 Kaumuali'i Hwy., #367, Waimea; (808) 338-1625/(877) 997-6667/*www.waimea-plantation.com* or *www.aston-hotels.com*. 46 units, located on the beach. TV, phones, kitchens; swimming pool, and tennis and volleyball courts. Handicap facilities. Minimum stay, 3 days.

Dining | Hanapepe, Waimea, Koke'e

[Restaurant prices—based on full course dinner, excluding drinks, tax and tips—are categorized as follows: *Deluxe*, over $30; *Expensive*, $20-$30; *Moderate*, $10-$20; *Inexpensive*, under $10.]

Green Garden Restaurant. *Inexpensive-Moderate.* 13749 Kaumuali'i Hwy., Hanapepe; (808) 335-5422. Delightful garden setting, amid lush, tropical plants. Menu features primarily Continental cuisine, including fresh fish and steak; also homemade lilikoi pies. Cocktails. Open for breakfast, lunch and dinner. Reservations suggested.

Hanapepe Café. *Inexpensive.* 3830 Hanapepe Rd., Hanapepe; (808) 335-5011. Housed in historic, 1930s building, with an antique fountain counter that now serves as the espresso bar. The café offers homemade scones, freshly-baked croissants and waffles for breakfast, and gourmet vegetarian lunches featuring vegetarian pot pies and caesar salads. Also tropical fruit smoothies. Open for lunch Mon.-Fri., dinner on Fridays.

Koke'e Lodge. *Inexpensive.* Koke'e State Park, 3600 Koke'e Rd., Waimea; (808) 335-6061/*www.kokee-kauai.com*. Situated in Kauai's high country, overlooking a beautiful meadow. Menu features standard American fare and island favorites, including sandwiches, salads, breads, soups, chili, quiches, pies, and hot and cold beverages. Open 9 a.m.-5 p.m. daily.

Pacific Deli & Pizza. Inexpensive. 9852 Kaumuali'i Hwy., Waimea; (808) 338-1020. Casual eatery, featuring salads, sandwiches and pizza. Open for lunch and dinner daily.

Waimea Brewing Company. *Inexpensive-Moderate.* Located at the Waimea Plantation Cottages, 9400 Kaumuali'i Hwy., #367, Waimea; (808) 338-9733. Casual brew-pub serving hand-crafted beer and a selection of pupus (appetizers), including spicy chicken wings, quesadillas and calamari. Also on the menu are burgers, sandwiches, soups, salads, steak, ribs and kalua pig. Open for lunch and dinner daily.

EAST SIDE | 4

Wailua | Kapa'a | Waipouli | Anahola

The East Side of Kauai, also referred to as the Coconut Coast, is more populous—and more fertile—than the West Side and even the South Shore of the island. It takes in, quite broadly, the area extending northward along the east coast of Kauai, from just above Lihue to Moloa'a Bay at the northeastern corner of the island. The principal towns here are Wailua and Kapa'a, and the area also includes the tourist-alluring Fern Grotto as well as one of Hawaii's largest coconut groves.

Wailua   8 *See Map 8 on Page 51*

Wailua River State Park

Lydgate State Park, Fern Grott, Smith's Tropical Paradise

The first place of note on the East Side of Kauai is Wailua, one of the oldest towns on this part of the island. It is situated some 6 miles north of Lihue on Kuhio Highway (56), at the mouth of the Wailua River—Hawaii's only navigable river, the source of which is Mount Wai'ale'ale (elevation, 5,148 feet) at the center of the island, notable as the wettest spot on earth. The low-lying coastal area surrounding the Wailua River, where the river drains into the ocean, was once one of the most sacred places in Hawaii, dotted with scores of *heiaus* and places of refuge—there are seven sacred *heiaus* still there—from where the *ali'i* (chiefs) would make their pilgrimage along the river to the altar at the top of Wai'ale'ale. The area is now part of the **Wailua River State Park**, a popular recreational park that offers good waterskiing, kayaking and fishing possibilities. Incidentally, Wailua River State Park takes in Lydgate State Park, parts of the Wailua River bank, Fern Grotto, and most of the *heiaus* in the area.

▶   At **Lydgate State Park**—located on the coast just to the south of
the mouth of the Wailua River, and reached on Kuhio Highway (56)
north from Lihue some 5 miles, then off on Leho Drive, a half mile,
to Nalu Road, which leads directly to the park—there are good
swimming, picnicking, fishing and beachcombing possibilities,
making it especially attractive for family recreation. The beach here
offers some of the safest swimming conditions on the island, with
a boulder breakwater built to protect it from the shorebreak. Also,
a little way north along the beach at Lydgate Park, you can visit
the site of the **Hauola Place of Refuge**, marked by a plaque, where
breakers of *kapu* would go to atone for their sins before being permitted back into society.

Just south of the Wailua River, too, on the *mauka*—inland—side
of Kuhio Highway (56), is the Wailua Marina, from where cruise
boats depart daily, up the Wailua River, for the much-publicized
Fern Grotto—an amphitheater-like cave, with huge, overhanging ferns inside it, and which also produces some extraordinarily
wonderful acoustics. Fern Grotto is also the setting for hundreds of
weddings each year, and the boat trips, typically, feature live Hawaiian music, including in their score the *Hawaiian Wedding Song*
and other Hawaiian melodies.

Also at the Wailua Marina is **Smith's Tropical Paradise**, a 30-
acre cultural and botanical garden, where self-guided tours lead
down paths criss-crossing the gardens, past a variety of exotic
plants, flowers and trees of Kauai. There are also Japanese, Filipino
and Polynesian villages built on the grounds here, celebrating the
cultural and ethnic mix of the people of Kauai; and each night,
a garden luau and international show highlights the foods and
entertainment of Tahiti, Hawaii, China, Japan, the Philippines, New
Zealand and Samoa.

North from Wailua River

*Wailua Beach Park,
Marriott Kauai*

North of the mouth of the Wailua River lies the **Wailua Beach Park**,
a half-mile-long beach, extending north from the river mouth to a
rocky point on the coast, alongside the highway (56). Wailua Beach
is a popular beach, although swimming is not encouraged here due
to the strong rip tides at various points along this coast, especially
near the mouth of the river.

On the *mauka*—inland—side of Wailua Beach Park is the site
of the old **Coco Palms Hotel**, which was severely damaged by the
hurricane Iniki in 1992. It is significant in that it was originally built
in 1953 on the site of an ancient royal court, and quickly came to
epitomize Hawaiiana, providing the setting for such early Holly-
wood hits as *South Pacific, Blue Hawaii*, starring Elvis Presley, and

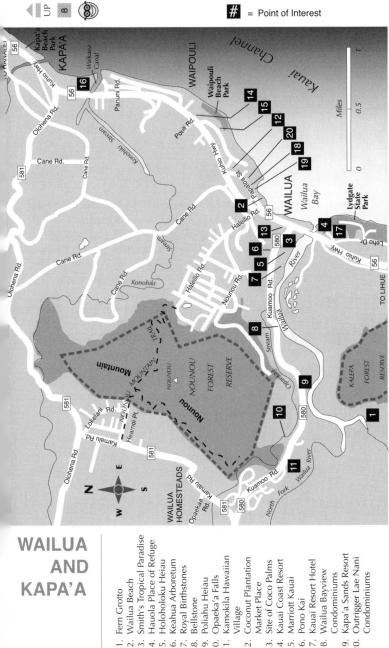

 # = Point of Interest

WAILUA AND KAPA'A

EAST SIDE | Wailua

Sadie Thompson, starring Rita Hayworth.

15 Another resort of interest in the area, the **Courtyard by Marriott Kauai**, is located just to the northeast of the Coco Palms site on Kuhio Highway. The Marriott resort is set amid 11 acres of towering coconut palms along Waipouli Beach, and boasts 309 rooms in a multi-winged building. Yet another resort hotel of note here is the 243-room Kauai Coast Resort, situated among coconut palms along a 1-mile stretch of Waipouli Beach.

Inland from Wailua

Poliahu Heiau, Opaeka'a Falls, Kamokila Hawaiian Village Keahua Arboretum

West from Wailua, a worthwhile detour leads directly inland along Highway 580, journeying alongside the Wailua River, past a handful of archaeological sites, to the Opaeka'a Falls and, farther, to the Keahua Arboretum. At the very outset, however, roughly three quarters of a mile from the Kuhio Highway intersection, is the **Poaiahu Arboretum**, featuring a small stand of trees, located alongside the highway; and directly across the highway from there is the ancient

5 **Holoholoku Heiau**, a temple of human sacrifice for those unfortunate enough to fail to escape to the nearby Hauola Place of Refuge.

7 Also near the arboretum and Holoholoku Heiau are the **Royal Birthstones**, Pohaku Ho'o Hanau, where, we are told, mothers of royal lineage would go to give birth to their babies—future kings and queens, no less. Following the birth of the child, the child's umbilical cord would be wedged into a crack in another sacred stone here, Pohaku Piko, to foretell the child's future: typically, if the cord was eaten up by a rat, the child, sadly, would become a thief; if not, glory to the child, for he would become a prosperous *ali'i*—or chief. Also, in accordance with a long-standing custom, the newborn *ali'i* would be carried by *kahunas* (Hawaiian priests)—in order that the

8 baby's feet not touch the ground—up the river to a **bellstone** which, when struck in the appropriate manner, would resound throughout the valley, alerting all the inhabitants of the area to the arrival of the newborn *ali'i*. The bellstone, of course, is located just east of the Poliahu Heiau, off Highway 580, at the end of a dirt road. From there you can also enjoy good, commanding views of the Wailua River and the Pacific Ocean beyond.

Close at hand, too, located on the south side of the highway,

9 just before reaching the Opaeka'a Falls, is the **Poliahu Heiau**, a personal temple of the ruling chiefs, built, it is believed, by Kauai's mysterious little people, the *menehune*. The *heiau*, named for the Hawaiian goddess of snow, Poliahu, is situated on a hill overlooking the surrounding valleys and the Wailua River, and, farther out, the Pacific Ocean.

Farther still, nearly 2 miles from the Kuhio Highway (56) turnoff, are the well-visited **Opaeka'a Falls**, wide, and cascading some 40 feet. Also, a little way from the waterfalls lies the **Kamokila Hawaiian Village**, a recreated Hawaiian village that is open to public viewing. Informative guided tours lead past thatched huts and a variety of native plants and trees—including patches of *taro*, from which the Hawaiian staple, *poi*, is made—explaining to visitors the applied uses for each. The ancient crafts of weaving mats and skirts are also demonstrated here.

Finally, another 4 or 5 miles—almost 7 miles from the Kuhio Highway turnoff—is the **Keahua Arboretum**, which is in fact part of the U.S. Forest Preserve. This is a lovely, secluded area, ideal for picnicking, with the Keahua Stream affording abundant opportunities for swimming. There are also some good hiking possibilities here, including a half-mile trail that loops through groves of eucalyptus and monkey pod trees, as well as a scenic, 2-mile trail that journeys over the Kuilau Ridge. Also of interest, 150 yards or so from the parking area, is a natural pool, ideal for swimming, with a rope tied to an overhanging branch of a tree, enabling you to swing out over the water.

North from Wailua

See Map 8
on Page 51

Waipouli and Nounou Mountain

Immediately north of Wailua lies the tiny community of Waipouli, which has as its chief—perhaps only—attraction, the **Coconut Plantation Marketplace**, situated on the *makai*—ocean—side of the Kuhio Highway (56), about a mile from the Coco Palms hotel in Wailua. The Coconut Plantation Marketplace offers excellent shopping possibilities, with a myriad shops and boutiques, retailing everything from the rare, expensive Ni'ihau shell leis to relatively inexpensive clothing and souvenirs. There are also some worthwhile eateries and restaurants here, as well as a theater, and on Wednesdays a popular, free-of-charge, Polynesian-style hula show is featured at the marketplace.

Just north from Waipouli, too, from Kipuni Place, on the west side of the highway (56), you can view the **Nounou Mountain Range**, also known as the "Sleeping Giant." Legend endures that the huge giant once lay asleep, in the very same place that he now lies now, while the island of Kauai was being invaded; and the *menehune* tried in vain to awaken him, throwing rocks at him, which bounced off the giant and landed on the invading army, eventually defeating it. Some of the rocks, however, as the *menehune* later discovered, had lodged in the giant's throat, thus killing him in his sleep.

EAST SIDE | Wailua

In any case, there are two separate trails leading to the summit of Nounou Mountain, climbing more than 1,000 feet, and with good, all-round views of the surrounding area. The east-side trail-head, which is approximately 2 miles from the summit, is located just off Haleilio Road, a mile west of Kuhio Highway in Wailua; and the west-side trail, which journeys roughly one and one-half miles to the top of the mountain, begins a quarter of a mile north of mile marker 4 on Kamalu Road (Highway 581), which goes off Kuamo'o Road (Highway 580).

Kapa'a

Kapa'a Beach Park, Kealia Beach, Donkey Beach

  8

See Map 8 on Page 51

Kapa'a lies approximately 2 miles north of Wailua (or 8 miles north of Lihue) on Kuhio Highway (56). It is a former sugar and pine-apple plantation town that has emerged as Kauai's most populous community, ahead of even Lihue, with a population of over 8,000. The town is filled with several restored, 19th-century storefronts and buildings, housing, quite typically, souvenir and clothing shops and other tourist-oriented businesses. In addition to its town center, Kapa'a also has some good beaches: on Niu Road, which goes off Kuhio Highway, heading north, is **Kapa'a Beach Park**, a narrow, sandy beach that primarily attracts fishermen as well as some dedicated swimmers; and just to the north of there, also alongside Kuhio Highway, lie several more, quite lovely beaches.

North from Kapa'a, Kuhio Highway (56) journeys through sugar-cane fields and wide-open spaces, passing by, just out from town, a lookout with spectacular views of the east coast of the island. Also, some 2 miles from Kapa'a, at mile marker 10, is **Kealia Beach**, situated alongside the highway. Kealia is a delightful, crescent-shaped, sandy beach, stretching approximately a half mile between two rocky points, especially popular with surfing and bodysurfing enthusiasts. However, swimming is inadvisable here for the most part, primarily due to the strong, unsafe ocean currents; although, during calm weather, a small jetty at the north end of the beach offers a somewhat protected area for swimming.

North from Kealia Beach, a little over one and one-half miles, lies **Donkey Beach**, a picturesque, crescent-shaped, windswept beach, surrounded by ironwoods, naupaka and ilima, tucked away from the highway, with a well-worn trail leading down from the highway to the beach. The beach is especially popular with nudists, even though nude bathing at public beaches in Hawaii is prohibited under state law. Interestingly, Donkey Beach is named for the mules—once mistaken for donkeys—seen grazing in the pasture directly behind the beach, used by the Lihue Plantation Company to carry cane seed and bags of fertilizer to the nearby fields.

Anahola | *Anahola Beach Park, Hole in the Mountain,*
Moloa'a Beach

Next up, another mile or so on Kuhio Highway, is Anahola, a small town bathed in fragrant plumeria, set aside, in part, for Hawaiian homesteads. The only place of visitor interest here, however, reached on Kukuihale Road—which goes off the highway at mile marker 13—is **Anahola Beach Park**, a long, thin beach, bordered by ironwoods, and which also has some picnic tables and restroom facilities. There is a safe swimming area here, protected by a reef, but when the surf is up, dangerous undercurrents can occur, making swimming in these waters inadvisable.

A little farther, just north of mile marker 15, looking toward the mountains you can see the Anahola Mountain Range, and through it, the **Hole-in-the-Mountain**, now almost closed by a landslide, but with a patch of daylight still showing through. Legend has it that the hole was created when a fierce warrior, engaged in battle with another warrior, flung his spear in fury, all the way from Koloa, piercing the mountains here, with the spear eventually landing farther northwest in Hanalei.

At any rate, northward, approximately a half mile past mile marker 16 on Kuhio Highway, at the corner of Ko'olau Road, is the Sunrise Fruit Stand, where you can sample fresh island fruit as well as delicious fruit smoothies; and a little way from there, at the end of Moloa'a Road—which goes off Ko'olau Road, just over a mile from the fruit stand—lies **Moloa'a Beach**, an idyllic, crescent-shaped beach, thoroughly secluded, and a great place for beachcombing and collecting sea shells. And again, a word of caution—the prevailing rip tides and a shore break make the ocean here rather unsafe for swimming.

Accommodations | **Wailua, Kapa'a**

Hotels

Aston Islander on the Beach. *$156-$265*. 440 Aleka Pl., Kapa'a; (808) 822-7417/(877) 997-6667/*www.aston-hotels.com*. Oceanfront hotel with 196 units, some with ocean views and some with garden views. TV, phones, refrigerators, wet bars, air conditioning, private balconies. Also swimming pool, restaurant and cocktail lounge on premises. Golf course, public tennis courts and shops nearby.

Courtyard by Marriott Kauai at Waipouli Beach. *$159-$335*. 4-484 Kuhio Hwy., Kapa'a; (808) 822-3455/(800) 760-8555/*www.marriotthawaii.com/waipouli.html*. Oceanfront hotel situated in historic Coconut Plantation. 311 air-conditioned units with TV, phones, refrigerators, wireless internet. Also freshwater pool, exercise room, and restaurant on premises. Handicap facilities.

Hotel Coral Reef. *$49-$89*. 4-1516 Kuhio Hwy., Kapa'a; (808) 822-4481/(800) 843-4659. 28 units in beachfront hotel. Complimentary breakfast. Handicapped facilities.

Kauai Sands Hotel. $90-$165. 420 Papaloa Rd., Kapa'a; (808) 822-4951/(800) 560-5553/*wwwkauaisandshotel.com*. Situated on the beachside of the Coconut Plantation. 50 rooms, some with kitchenettes. Complimentary breakfast. Also shops, restaurant and lounge.

Condominiums

Aloha Beach Resort. *$150-$280*. 3-5920 Kuhio Hwy., Kapa'a; (808) 823-6000/(888) 823-5111/*www.abrkauai.com*. 216 units, including ocean- and garden-view rooms, 1-bedroom suites, and 2-room cottages. Located adjacent to Lydgate Beach. Two swimming pools, jacuzzi, fitness room, tennis court, volleyball court and shuffleboard court. TV, phone, refrigerator, safe. Restaurant, lounge, snack bar and delicatessen.

Kapa'a Sands Resort. *$85-$129*. 380 Papaloa Rd., Kapa'a; (808) 822-4901/(800) 222-4901/*www.kapaasands.com*. 24 oceanfront condominium units, including studios and 2-bedroom units. Phones; swimming pool.

Kauai Coast Resort at the Beachboy. *$185-$275*. 520 Aleka Loop, Kapa'a; (808) 822-3441/(800) 364-4043/(800) 367-7052/ *www.kauaicoastresort.com*. 94 one- and two-bedroom units in oceanfront condominium complex. TV, phones, kitchens, laundry facilities, lanais; also hot tub, exercise room, tennis court, and restaurant and cocktail lounge on premises.

Outrigger Lae Nani. *$195-$295*. 410 Papaloa Rd., Kapa'a; (808) 822-4938/(800) 777-1700/*www.outrigger.com*. 52 beachfront condominium units, with TV, phones, ceiling fans and kitchens. Swimming pool, tennis court. Daily maid service. Handicapped facilities.

Plantation Hale (Best Western). *$115-$150*. 484 Kuhio Hwy., Kapa'a; (808) 822-4941/(800) 775-4253/**733-7777**/*www.plantation-hale.com*. On the beach. 152 units in beachfront condominium complex. TV, phones, air conditioning and kitchen facilities. Swimming pool, spa, barbecue area. Restaurant and cocktail lounge, and shops nearby.

Pono Kai Resort. *$89-$229*. 4-1250 Kuhio Hwy., Kapa'a; (808) 822-9831/(800) 922-7866/*www.ponokai-resort.com*. 217-unit beachfront condominium complex, with one- and two-bedroom units. TV, phones, kitchens, and laundry facilities. Swimming pool, spa, sauna, tennis courts, shuffleboard; also barbecue area.

Wailua Bay View Condominiums. *$125-$150.* 320 Papaloa Rd., Kapa'a; (425) 391-0207/(800) 882-9007/*www.wailuabay.com*. 40 one-bedroom oceanfront condominium units, with TV, phones, microwave ovens and laundry facilities; some with air-conditioning. Swimming pool and barbecue area.

Hostel

Kauai International Hostel. *$20-$50.* 4532 Lehua St., Kapa'a; (808) 823-6142/(808) 821-9813/*www.kauaihostel.net*. Guest house and hostel, with 40 dormitory units and 5 private units. Shared kitchen, bathroom, TV and phone. Daily island excursions offered.

Bed and Breakfast

Hale Lani Bed & Breakfast. *$105-$150.* 283 Aina Lani Pl., Kapa'a, HI 96746; (808) 823-6434/(877) 423-6434/*www.hale-lani.com*. Offers 4 self-contained, individually-decorated, private accommodations, including two studios, a two-bedroom suite and a cottage, all with fully equipped kitchens and baths, private entrances, private patios, queen beds, TV, phones, stereos, fresh flowers and bottled water. Tropical garden setting. Full Hawaiian breakfast. Weekly rates: $630-$900. Minimum stay, 3 nights.

Kauai Country Inn. *$95-$250.* 6440 Olohena Rd., Kapa'a, HI 96746; (808) 821-0207/*www.kauaicountryinn.com*. Situated on 2-acre tropical estate on Kauai's East Side, amid guava, passion fruit and mango trees. Offers four tastefully-furnished, Hawaiian-decor one- and two-bedroom suites and one country cottage, all with private baths and fully-equipped kitchen facilities; also TVs, DVD players and computers with DSL internet access. Tea room and private Beatles museum on premises. Fresh, island breakfast.

Lani Keha Bed & Breakfast. *$55-$80.* 848 Kamalu Road, Kapa'a, HI 96746; (808) 822-1605/(800) 821-4898/*www.lanikeha.com*. Located on three acres nestled up against the Sleeping Giant Mountain. 3 bedrooms with TV, VCR, and private baths. Whole house also available for rental, at $250.00 per night.

Mohala Ke Ola Bed & Breakfast. *$100-$125.* 5663 Ohelo Rd., Kapa'a, HI 96746; (808) 823-6398/(888) 465-2824/*www.waterfallbnb.com*. Home in secluded setting, backing onto state forest land and the Wailua River Valley. 4 large guest rooms with private baths, ceiling fans, and mountain and waterfall views. Jacuzzi and pool on premises. Full breakfast with fresh island fruit.

EAST SIDE | Dining

Dining | Wailua, Waipouli, Kapa'a

[Restaurant prices—based on full course dinner, excluding drinks, tax and tips—are categorized as follows: *Deluxe*, over $30; *Expensive*, $20-$30; *Moderate*, $10-$20; *Inexpensive*, under $10.]

Aloha Kauai Pizza. *Inexpensive.* Located in the Coconut Marketplace, 4-484 Kuhio Hwy., Waipouli; (808) 822-4511. Pizza, lasagna, calzone, salads, sandwiches and fresh breads. Open 11 a.m.- 9 p.m. daily.

Bubba's Burgers. *Inexpensive.* 4421 Kuhio Hwy., Kapa'a; (808) 823-0069. Casual burger joint overlooking Kapa'a Beach Park. Open daily from 10.30 a.m.-8 p.m.

Bull Shed. *Moderate.* 796 Kuhio Hwy., Waipouli; (808) 822-3791. Oceanview restaurant, featuring fresh seafood, chicken, steak, lobster, and rack of lamb served in traditional American or Polynesian style. Salad bar. Open for dinner. Reservations recommended.

Buzz's Steak & Lobster. *Moderate.* At the Coconut Marketplace, 484 Kuhio Hwy., Waipouli; (808) 822-0041. Polynesian-decor steak house. Offers a variety of steaks and fresh island seafood. House specialties include deep-fried calamari and Seafood Brochette. Salad bar. Entertainment. Open for lunch and dinner daily.

Hanama'ulu Restaurant and Tea House. *Moderate.* 3-4291 Kuhio Hwy., Hanama'ulu; (808) 245-2511. Delightful setting amid Japanese gardens and ponds. Offers primarily Japanese and Chinese cuisine, including tempura, sushi, chop suey and beef broccoli. Private tea rooms available. Open for lunch and dinner. Reservations suggested.

King and I. *Moderate.* 4-901 Kuhio Hwy., Waipouli; (808) 822-1642. Authentic Thai cuisine. Specialties include sah-teh and fried calamari; also chicken and fresh fish curries, and daily vegetarian specials. Open for lunch Mon.-Fri., dinner daily. Reservations suggested.

Kountry Kitchen. *Inexpensive.* 1485 Kuhio Hwy., Kapa'a; (808) 822-3511. Home-style American eatery, serving a variety of omelettes, banana pancakes, eggs, steak, pork chops, fresh fish, hamburgers and salads. Open for breakfast and lunch daily.

Mema. *Moderate.* 4-369 Kuhio Hwy., Kapa'a; (808) 823-0899. Good selection of Thai and Chinese dishes; also large selection of vegetarian items. House specialties include Pad Thai and cashew nut chicken. Open for lunch and dinner daily.

Mermaid Café. *Moderate.* 4-1384 Kuhio Hwy., Kapa'a; (808) 821-2026.Casual café, offering healthful foods, including spinach tortilla chicken wraps and burritos; also island-style coconut curry and organic wild rice plates. Open for breakfast, lunch and dinner, Mon.-Sat.

Norberto's El Café. *Inexpensive-Moderate.* 4-1373 Kuhio Hwy., Kapa'a; (808) 822-3362. Traditional Mexican food, including meat and vegetarian enchiladas grande, burritos and fajitas. Complimentary nachos with fresh, hot salsa. Spanish decor. Open for dinner daily (except Sundays).

Ono Family Restaurant. *Inexpensive.* 4-1292 Kuhio Hwy., Kapa'a; (808) 822-1710. American and island specialties—sandwiches, burgers, top sirloin, barbecued ribs, buffalo cube steak, mahi mahi, and shrimp plates. Open for breakfast and lunch daily.

A Pacific Café. *Moderate-Expensive.* 4-831 Kuhio Hwy., Suite 220, Waipouli; (808) 822-0013. Contemporary setting. Specializing in Pacific Rim cuisine with a European flare. Menu features fresh island fish cooked over a wood-burning grill, pasta, sirloin steak, and roast Chinese duck, served with an array of unique sauces. Open for dinner. Reservations recommended.

Panda Garden Chinese Restaurant. *Moderate.* 4-831 Kuhio Hwy., Waipouli; (808) 822-0092. Traditional Chinese cuisine, with emphasis on Szechuan and Cantonese dishes. Lunch and dinner daily.

Restaurant Kintaro. *Moderate-Expensive.* 4-370 Kuhio Hwy., Wailua; (808) 822-3341. Japanese cuisine, featuring Teppan-style dinners, with chicken teriyaki, lobster tail, and filet mignon; also complete sushi bar. Traditional Japanese decor. Dinner daily. Reservations recommended.

Voyager Grille. *Expensive-Deluxe.* At the Marriott Kauai, 4-484 Kuhio Hwy., Kapa'a; (808) 822-6652/822-3455/(800) 760-8555. Island cuisine, with emphasis on fresh island fish, seafood and steak. Menu also features prime rib, chicken, filet mignon, rack of lamb, soups, salads and a Hawaiian Luau Platter. Open for breakfast, lunch and dinner. Reservations recommended.

Wailua Marina Restaurant. *Moderate.* Located in the Wailua River State Park, 5971 Kuhio Hwy., Wailua; (808) 822-4311. Steaks and seafood, including Hawaiian spiny lobster tail and char-broiled mahi mahi, and barbecued ribs. Outdoor dining, on lanai overlooking Wailua River. Lunch and dinner, Tues.-Sun. Reservations suggested.

EAST SIDE | Dining

NORTH SHORE | 5

Kilauea | Princeville | Hanalei | Ha'ena | Lumahai Beach | Ke'e Beach Park

The North Shore of Kauai, for all practical purposes, begins near Kepuhi Point, just east of Kilauea, and takes in the lush, green northern portion of the island, across to Ke'e Beach at the northeastern end of the Na Pali Coast. It includes in it, besides Kilauea, the Princeville-Hanalei area, the tiny villages of Wainiha and Ha'ena, and Lumahai Beach, one of Hawaii's most famous beaches.

Kilauea

Waiakalua Iki and Waiakalua Nui Beaches, Christ Memorial Episcopal Church, Kung Lung Company Building

Kilauea

Kilauea is the first town reached on Kauai's North Shore when journeying from the East Side. It is situated on the northeast corner of the island, some 15 miles from Kapa'a (or 23 miles from Lihue) on Kuhio Highway (56). But before Kilauea, there are two beaches of interest—**Waiakalua Iki Beach** and **Waiakalua Nui Beach**, reached by way of North Waiakalua Road, which goes off the highway toward the ocean, some three quarters of a mile past mile marker 20, then left at the end of Waiakalua Road onto a dirt road, another quarter mile or so to the end, from where a short, steep trail leads down to Waiakalua Iki Beach, with Waiakalua Nui Beach adjoining to the west of it. Waiakalua Iki and Waiakalua Nui beaches are both quite scenic, in secluded settings, and offer good beachcombing possibilities. Swimming is not encouraged at either of them, however, mainly due to the abundant coral and unpredictable ocean currents.

In any case, Kilauea is a former sugar plantation town, founded in the late 1870s by the Kilauea Sugar Plantation Company, which operated here for nearly a century, until 1970. The town is small, rural, and filled with plantation-era buildings—all, surprisingly, built from stone, constituting what is considered to be the most extensive use of lava rock in the islands. Among the best examples of this rock construction is the **Christ Memorial Episcopal Church**, a quaint, coral rock church, dating from 1941 and featuring a hand-carved altar and stained-glass windows imported from England. The church is located on Kolo Road, which goes off Kuhio Highway, a quarter mile or so past mile marker 23. Another, the **Kong Lung Company Building**, also built from lava rock in 1941, is located on Kilauea Road, heading *makai*—toward the ocean.

Around Kilauea | *Kilauea Point Wildlife Refuge, Kilauea Lighthouse, Guava Plantation, Quarry Beach, Secret Beach, Kalihiwai Valley Overlook, Anini Beach Park*

Besides the immediate town, Kilauea has one or two other points of interest quite close to it. Just to the north of town, for instance, at the end of Kilauea Road is the **Kilauea Point National Wildlife Refuge**, a splendid, 160-acre coastal park that includes in it Kilauea Point—the northernmost point on Kauai, and consequently in the state of Hawaii—and the 568-foot Crater Hill and Molokea Point, lying just to the east. The wildlife refuge itself is a nesting colony for endangered seabirds, including red-footed boobies, wedge-tailed shearwaters, laysan albatross and the great frigate birds, all of which can be seen here, along this rugged coastline, from Kilauea Point. From here, too, it is possible to see various marine life, especially during the winter and spring months, including whales, dolphins, seals and sea turtles. Also of interest at the reserve, located at Kilauea Point, is the old **Kilauea Lighthouse**, originally built in 1913. It once featured a 4-ton Fresnel Lens, a beacon for passing ships for some 67 years, until it was finally replaced in 1980 by a smaller, more powerful light. The lighthouse is now a National Historic Landmark.

Two other places of visitor interest in the Kilauea area are the **Guava Kai Plantation** and **Banana Joe's**. The first of these, the Guava Kai Plantation, located on Kuawa Road—which goes off Kuhio Highway westward—comprises 480 acres of guava orchards, where the public can not only tour the orchards and guava processing plant, but also sample and buy a variety of guava products, including guava muffins, sherbets, sweet rolls, jams, jellies, and juice. At Banana Joe's—which is located just to the west of town, roughly a quarter mile inland from Kuhio Highway—you can also sample some local products, including locally-grown fruit, fresh coconut milk, and fruit smoothies.

There are a handful of beaches of interest near Kilauea as well. The first, Kahili Beach, also known as **Quarry Beach**—named for a nearby quarry—can be reached by way of Kilauea Road, a quarter mile or so north of the Kong Lung Center, then off on an unmarked, four-wheel-drive-only dirt road, eastward another one and one-half miles, to the beach. Quarry Beach is quite popular with surfers and fishermen, where you can frequently watch the fishermen casting their out-size nets. Swimming, however, is not encouraged here, except in calm seas, due to the prevailing rip tides.

Another beach, Kauapea Beach, popularly known as **Secret Beach**—even though everyone knows about it—lies more or less directly to the northwest of Kilauea. It can be reached on Kuhio Highway, west from the town a half mile or so, then Kalihiwai Road a little way to a dirt road, which heads out north to the beach parking area, from where a well-worn trail leads down to the beach.

Secret Beach is a long, wide, white-sand beach, picturesque and secluded, extending from Kilauea Point westward, and increasingly popular with nudists—even though nude bathing at public beaches is prohibited in the state of Hawaii. And again, as with other beaches on the North Shore, swimming is not advised due to the strong undercurrents and high surf, especially during winter and spring months.

Also along Kalihiwai Road is Kalihiwai Beach, a wide, sandy beach, bordered by ironwood trees. Kalihiwai is quite popular with surfers, particularly due to its shorebreak and excellent surf—which, conversely, are detrimental to swimming, making it rather unsafe for the latter. For kayakers, however, there is the Kalihiwai River, which winds past several sparkling waterfalls, ultimately draining into the ocean near the west end of the beach.

Westward from Kilauea also, one and one-half miles on Kuhio ▶ Highway (56), at mile marker 25, is the **Kalihiwai Valley Overlook**, with sweeping views of Kalihiwai Valley, dotted with waterfalls, and the Kalihiwai River below. A little way east from the overlook on the highway, too, you can view a magnificent waterfall on the *mauka*—inland—side of the road.

Westward still, a half mile or so along Anini Road—which goes off Kalihiwai Road, which, in turn, goes off Kuhio Highway west- ▶ ward, roughly a half mile past mile marker 25—is **Anini Beach Park**, a surprisingly popular beach, protected by one of the longest and widest reefs in the islands, some 2 miles long, and lying a quarter mile or so offshore. The beach park has picnic tables, some of them sheltered, as well as showers and restroom facilities. The beach also offers good windsurfing, snorkeling, fishing and beachcombing possibilities. Also, directly across from the park, on the opposite side of Anini Road, are the Polo Grounds, where polo matches are played on Sundays during spring and summer months.

Princeville and Hanalei

See Map 9
on Page 65

Princeville

Princeville Hotel, Hanalei Bay Resort,

Princeville, situated some 28 miles north of Lihue on Kauai's north shore, is a major resort development, with luxury hotels and con-dominiums and an exclusive residential community, sprawled on 11,000 acres of prime, oceanfront land, overlooking Hanalei Bay, backed by the Hanalei Valley, and the Pacific Ocean. Interestingly, in 1860, a pioneer settler named Robert C. Wyllie acquired the Princeville acreage and attempted to establish a sugar plantation, but quickly found the climate to be too wet and cool and utterly unsuited to the cultivation of sugarcane. In any case, Wyllie, follow-ing a visit by King Kamehameha IV and his wife, Queen Emma, to-gether with their 2-year-old son, Prince Ka Haku o Hawaii, named the resort "Princeville," in honor of the young prince.

At the heart of Princeville, of course, is the multi-million-dollar **Princeville Hotel**, situated on the lookout point at Hanalei Bay, Pu'u Poa Point, and built in descending tiers down the face of a cliff. The hotel, originally developed in 1985 and renovated in 1989 at a cost of $120 million, boasts 252 luxury guest rooms with views, three well-appointed restaurants, trendy shops and boutiques, an Olympic-size swimming pool, more than 20 tennis courts, and an in-house, 64-seat cinema where you can watch—what else?—re-runs of *South Pacific*, the 1950s classic, and *From Here To Eternity*, among others. Near the Princeville Hotel, too, are two world-class golf courses—the famous, 27-hole Makai Course, ranked among the top 100 courses in the country by *Golf Digest*; and the recently-completed Prince Course, a championship, 18-hole course—both designed by Robert Trent Jones, Jr., who, by the way, maintains a home in nearby Hanalei.

Princeville's other major development is the **Hanalei Bay Resort**, with 200 luxury units, nestled in 2- and 3-story buildings, overlook-ing historic Hanalei Bay and the ocean. The Hanalei Bay Resort also has in it a gourmet restaurant—which features traditional Hawai-ian luaus on certain nights of the week—and well-stocked shops, a sand-bottom pool, a dozen or so tennis courts, and golf at the nearby Princeville Resort golf courses. There are, besides, one or two other condominium complexes here as well, with good, com-fortable accommodations, and a small commuter airport, located just off the Kuhio Highway (56) on the *mauka*—inland—side of the road.

Princeville also has two beaches of interest—Sea Lodge Beach and Pu'u Poa Beach. Sea Lodge Beach comprises a small, secluded cove, reached by way of Kamehameha Road—which goes off Kahaku Road, the main road leading into Princeville from Kuhio

Highway—to the very end, at the Sea Lodge Condominiums, from where a short walk leads past the condominiums—between blocks B and C, and around block A, on the ocean side—following the coastline west, and so to the beach. The second beach, Pu'u Poa Beach, one of the most popular in the Princeville area, is situated more or less at the foot of the Princeville Hotel, with a public right-of-way leading down to the beach. Pu'u Poa Beach itself is a long, sandy beach, protected by a fringe reef, which makes this an especially good place for snorkeling in calm seas.

Hanalei

Hanalei Wildlife Refuge, Wai'oli Hui'ia Church, Wai'oli Museum, Hanalei Beach, Bali Hai, Wai'oli Beach

See Map 9 on Page 65

West from Princeville, at mile marker 28, Kuhio Highway (56) becomes Highway 560—with the mileage markers beginning again from 0—and a little way from there, on the *mauka*—inland—side of the highway is the **Hanalei Valley Lookout**, overlooking the fertile Hanalei Valley, 6 miles long and one mile wide, covered with fields of *taro*, the Hawaiian staple. Here, too, in the Hanalei Valley is the 917-acre **Hanalei National Wildlife Refuge**, established in 1972 as a sanctuary for indigenous water birds. Besides which, looking down from the overlook you can also see the Hanalei River below, crossed over by an arched, one-lane highway bridge, the **Hanalei Bridge**, built in 1912, which leads into Hanalei.

Hanalei itself is situated approximately a mile west from the Hanalei Bridge, at the head of Hanalei Bay. It is a typical North Shore town, rural, unhurried, and set in lush, green surroundings. It has in it several small shops, a handful of restaurants, one or two museums, and a church with historic interest, the **Wai'oli Hui'ia Church**, located just west of mile marker 3 on the *mauka* (inland) side of the highway (560). The Wai'oli Hui'ia Church was originally built in 1834 by Reverend William P. Alexander and his wife, Mary Ann—notably the first missionaries to arrive in Hanalei—and rebuilt in 1912. Also, just to the back of the church is the **Wai'oli Mission House Museum**, housed in the former home of missionaries Abner and Lucy Wilcox. The Mission House, characteristic in its New England architecture, was originally built in 1837—also by Reverend William P. Alexander and his wife—and restored in 1921 by the Wilcox' granddaughters, with the original missionary furnishings, dating from the late 1800s, including antique *koa* furniture as well as the original wood-burning stove and bookcases lined with several volumes from Abner Wilcox' collection. The museum is open to public viewing.

At Hanalei, too, bordering Hanalei Bay, is a 2-mile-long crescent-shaped beach, the **Hanalei Pavilion Beach Park**, quite popular with picnickers as well as surfers, notable for its gigantic swells during the winter months. The beach is reached by way of Aku Road

UP 9

= Point of Interest

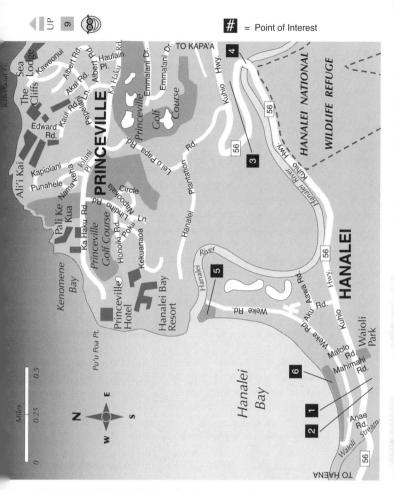

HANALEI AND PRINCEVILLE

1. Waioli Mission
2. Waioli Hui'ia Church
3. Hanalei Valley Lookout
4. Hanalei Bridge
5. Hanalei Beach Park
6. Waioli Beach Park

which goes off the highway (560) *makai*, then Weke Road which journeys along the periphery of the bay, with an access road on the right leading directly to the beach. From here also, you can see the northeast portion of the spectacular Na Pali Coast, as well as **Bali Hai**, the spire-like ridge rising just to the west of Hanalei Bay,. From here, too, you can enjoy some of the most beautiful sunsets on the island, as the sun goes down over the bay.

Also of interest, northward on Weke Road, at the very end of the road, is Black Pot Beach Park, situated at the mouth of the Hanalei River. Many of the cruise boats plying the Na Pali Coast depart from here as well, as do several kayaking trips heading up the Hanalei River. Besides which, **Black Pot Beach** is an excellent place to watch sunsets and the waves, and the dramatic mountains that form a backdrop for the sleepy little town of Hanalei. The beach, interestingly, is named for a black cooking pot that was once a fixture here, especially useful on occasions when local residents would gather at the beach to fish and socialize and add to the pot. There is also a restored, 100-year-old pier at the beach, which was once used for loading bags of rice—grown in the valley—onto boats waiting in the bay. It is now a popular place for pier fishing.

6   Try to also visit the **Wai'oli Beach Park**, also known as "Pine-trees," reached by way of Weke Road south a mile or so from Black Pot Beach, to He'e Road, which goes off toward the ocean to the beach park. The beach, incidentally, located at an approximate midway point along the bay, is bordered by ironwoods, not pine trees, contrary to what its name might suggest. The beach has good swimming possibilities in the summer months, when the ocean is calm; in winter and spring, however, the treacherous waves and dangerous rip tides make the area unsafe for the sport.

Westward on Highway 560 along the west side of Hanalei Bay, at mile marker 4, there is yet another beach, Waikoko Beach—a roadside beach bordered by ironwood trees and protected from the open ocean by a coral reef, making it ideally suited to family recreation. Although we must point out that the swimming area here, while safe and enjoyable for children, is much too shallow for adults.

Lumahai Beach to Ke'e Beach

See Map 10
on Page 68

Lumahai Beach

*Lumahai Beach, Tunnels Beach, Ha'ena
Beach Park, Ha'ena State Park, Dry Caves*

West still, a mile past mile marker 4, then off on a trail toward the ocean, passing through groves of pandanus trees—also known as screw pines and, often enough, as "tourist pineapple trees"—lies **Lumahai Beach**, the most beautiful of Kauai's beaches, made famous by the movie, *South Pacific*, filmed on location here in 1957. Not surprisingly, Lumahai is a also very popular day-use beach, three-quarters of a mile long, and sandy, with good swimming and snorkeling possibilities at its eastern end in the summer months, when the seas are calm. At the western end of the beach—where the Lumahai River drains into the ocean, and which is reached from the beach parking area, three quarter mile west of mile marker 5 on Kuhio Highway (560)—surfing and bodysurfing, at advanced levels, are the dominant sports. There is also an overlook here at mile marker 5, marked with a Hawaiian Visitors Bureau marker, with commanding views of Lumahai Beach.

West from Lumahai Beach, a half mile or so past mile marker 6, is the tiny village of Wainiha—meaning "unfriendly water"—the last place to obtain supplies before striking out farther west toward Ha'ena and the Na Pali Coast wilderness. West from Wainiha, too, another half mile, at mile marker 7, is Wainiha Beach, with its treacherous waters, where swimming is strongly discouraged.

Another nearby beach, **Tunnels Beach**, a rather popular beach that is protected by a large reef and offers a variety of activities, depending on the season and prevailing ocean conditions, is located some 2 miles or so to the west of Wainiha—a half mile past mile marker 8—with two separate access roads leading from the highway down to the beach. In calm weather, usually during the summer months, Tunnels Beach offers some of the best diving and snorkeling possibilities on the island; and in winter, when the ocean swells generate gigantic waves, the area draws world-class surfers to a point beyond the reef, known, simply, as "Tunnels." Tunnels Beach is also well liked by windsurfers when strong winds pick up.

A quarter mile west of Tunnels Beach lies **Ha'ena Beach Park**, with showers, restrooms and campsites, but largely unprotected from the ocean; and directly across from there, on the opposite side of the highway, is the **Maniniholo Dry Cave**, the first of three caves located alongside the highway here, a hundred yards deep and with a large opening. The Maniniholo Cave, we are told, was dug out by hand in ancient times, by a *menehune* fisherman searching for an evil spirit.

Westward from Ha'ena Beach is **Ha'ena State Park**, encompassing all of 230 acres. Besides archaeological sites, the park includes

NORTH SHORE | Lumahai Beach

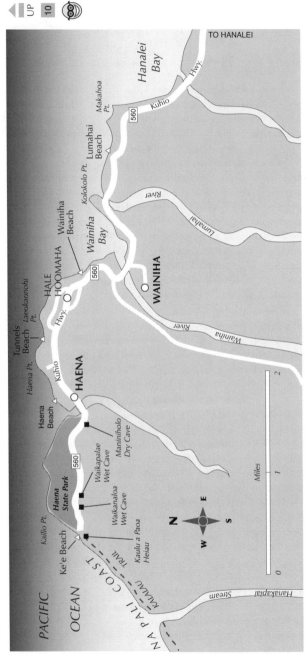

**LUMAHAI BEACH
AND KE'E BEACH**

the Waikanaloa and Waikapalae wet caves and Ke'e Beach. The **Waikanaloa** and **Waikapalae** caves are located just inside the park, on the *mauka*—inland—side of the highway, two-tenths and three-tenths of a mile from the park entrance, respectively. The caves are deep, dark and large, dug out, apparently, by Pele, the Hawaiian goddess of fire, in her relentless search for fire. Not surprisingly, all she found in the caves was water. Both caves are now well-visited North Shore landmarks.

Ke'e Beach

| Ke'e Beach, Ka'ulu Paoa Heiau, Kalalau Trailhead | | 10 | See Map 10 on Page 68 |

At mile marker 10—which is to say, approximately 8 miles from Hanalei, or 38 miles from Lihue—the road finally ends at **Ke'e Beach**, a popular swimming and snorkeling beach—in calm seas, that is—protected from the ocean by a large coral reef, and which also has showers and restroom facilities. From the western end of the beach, too, a trail journeys along the shoreline a little way, past the historic Allerton House—now a private residence—then up the hill to the ancient **Ka'ulu a Paoa Heiau**, situated in a grassy meadow, dedicated to Laka, the goddess of the *hula*. It is believed that it was here that Laka did much of her dancing. Dedicated students of the *hula* still make the pilgrimage to this ancient *heiau*, the most sacred shrine of the traditional Hawaiian dance of storytelling.

Nearby, at the Ke'e Beach parking lot is the **Kalalau Trail trailhead**, and just to its left, the site of the home of Lohiau, a legendary 16th century prince. It was here, we are told, that Pele, the goddess of fire, while searching for fire, was first distracted by the sound of the *hula* drums; and, upon seeing Lohiau, she instantly fell in love with him. But in her wisdom, she decided that she could not be his wife until she had found a suitable place to live; whereupon she continued her search, traveling to the other islands, finally settling in Kilauea, the mighty volcano in the center of the big island of Hawaii, where she found fire. With that settled, Pele then sent her sister, Hi'iaka, to bring Lohiau to Kilauea; but upon her arrival at Lohiau's home, Hi'iaka found the prince dead. Nevertheless, not one to give up easily, Hi'iaka located Lohiau's spirit and brought him back to life, and the two departed for Kilauea. As they approached Kilauea, however, Hi'iaka, overjoyed at having accomplished her mission, hugged and kissed Lohiau. The sight of this naturally sent Pele into a rage, and she ordered the death of Lohiau—to be buried in lava! But as it turned out, two of Pele's brothers, kind-hearted souls, discovered Lohiau in the lava and rescued and brought him back to Kauai, where he was reunited with Hi'iaka, and the two lived happily ever after—in Ha'ena. The site of Lohiau's house can still be seen here, identified as a low rock terrace that recedes into the mountains.

NORTH SHORE | Na Pali Coast

Na Pali Coast

The Kalalau Trail | Hanakapi'ai Beach, Hanakoa Valley

The Na Pali Coast is an astonishing, 15-mile coastal stretch along the northwestern end of the island—between Ke'e Beach and Polihale Beach—with steep, rugged cliffs plunging into the ocean, frequently overhung by ocean mist. The Na Pali Coast State Park, in fact, comprises some 6,000 acres of wild, unspoiled coastal terrain, with lush, verdant valleys and dramatic sea cliffs, accessible only on foot, or by boat or helicopter—except, of course, during flash floods and high surf, when it becomes completely inaccessible.

The best way to see the Na Pali Coast—other than cruising along its periphery or making a boat landing on one of its beaches—is on the rugged **Kalalau Trail**, which journeys from Ke'e Beach, winding some 11 miles along the wind- and wave-carved cliffs, to the ancient Kalalau Valley, at the ocean end of which lies the Kalalau Beach. However, we must point out that the Kalalau Trail is an arduous, challenging hike—8 to 10 hours each way—to be recommended only to the hardy souls. It is also possible to arrange for a drop off or pick up by boat at Kalalau Beach, thus enabling adventurers to hike the trail just one way. Additionally, camping is permitted at Kalalau Beach—as well as at Hanakapi'ai Beach and the Hanakoa Valley, which lie to the northeast of Kalalau Beach—with camping permits available from the Department of Land and Natural Resources in Lihue.

In any case, for those journeying from the northeast end of the Na Pali Coast, the Kalalau Trail sets out from Ke'e Beach and heads directly southwest, climbing approximately a mile, then descending another mile or so to the delightful **Hanakapi'ai Beach**, which has some picnicking and camping possibilities. Here also, just before reaching Hanakapi'ai Beach, a trail dashes off inland some 2 miles into the valley—passing by ancient rock-wall terraces that were once used to cultivate *taro*, as well as a deserted coffee mill—to the picturesque **Hanakapi'ai Falls**, cascading some 250 feet over the cliffs into a large pool, ideal for swimming. There are several other natural pools here, too, along the Hanakapi'ai Stream, all quite suitable for a refreshing little dip.

From Hanakapi'ai Beach it is another 4 miles or so, climbing and weaving around a series of switchbacks, and passing through the Ho'olulu and Waiahuakua valleys along the way—1 mile and 2½ miles from Hanakapi'ai Beach, respectively—to the lush, hanging **Hanakoa Valley**, which has camping possibilities as well as a handful of natural pools, dotted along the Hanakoa Stream, ideally suited to swimming. Here you can also visit the spectacular, 1,000-foot **Hanakoa Falls**, cascading in all their splendor into a large pool below, which, again, has good swimming possibilities. The falls are located roughly a third of a mile inside the valley, reached more or less directly on the trail leading into the valley.

Into Kalalau Valley

Kalalau Beach, Kalalau Valley, Waimakimaki Falls

Beyond Hanakoa Valley lies the Pohakuao Valley—comprising seven successive gulches—and some 5 miles from Hanakoa the Kalalau Trail finally ends at **Kalalau Beach**. Kalalau Beach itself is a secluded, sandy beach, approximately half mile long and some 80 yards wide, where camping is permitted and where you can also view one or two large sea caves as well as a 100-foot-long, 40-foot-wide *heiau*. From Kalalau Beach also, it is possible to hike inland a little way into the **Kalalau Valley**, a deep, broad valley, surrounded by 3,000- to 4,000-foot cliffs, and notable, too, as the site of an ancient Hawaiian settlement where native Hawaiians dwelled for centuries—until as recently as the 1920s!—with little or no contact with the outside world. Remnants of weathered rock-wall terraces are still visible here, once used by the ancient Hawaiians for cultivating taro. The valley is also abundant in fruit trees—guava, papaya, mango—and kukui nut trees. Besides which, it has in it a series of pools that are ideal for swimming, and the 250-foot **Waimakimaki Falls**—also known as Davis Falls—reached on a mile-long trail from the site of the settlement. As added interest, the Kalalau Valley also provided the setting for the remake of the film, *King Kong*.

Interestingly, in the late 1800s the Kalalau Valley was also used as a hideout by a Hawaiian named Ko'olau, who, we are told, having contracted leprosy, was sought out by the government for banishment to the leper colony on the remote Kalaupapa Peninsula on the island of Molokai. However, rather than be removed to the forlorn peninsula, Ko'olau fled with his wife and young son to the Kalalau Valley, where he eluded his captors for several years until, finally, he and his son—who, by then, had also developed symptoms of the disease—died in hiding. Ko'olau's wife, Pi'ilani, then buried her husband and son and, in great sorrow, emerged from the valley.

In any event, from the Kalalau Valley we must retrace our steps to Kalalau Beach and follow the Kalalau Trail northeastward to Hanakoa Valley, Hanakapi'ai Beach, and so to Ke'e Beach, our starting point.

NORTH SHORE | Na Pali Coast

NORTH SHORE | Accommodations

Accommodations | Princeville and Hanalei

Hotels

Hanalei Bay Resort. *$185-$390*. 5380 Honoiki Rd., Princeville; (808) 826-6522/(800) 827-4427/(877) 997-6667/(800) 922-7866/ *www.hanaleibayresort.com* or *www.aston-hotels.com*. 85 rooms, studios with kitchenettes, and suites with full kitchens. TV, phones, refrigerators, private lanais, and air conditioning. Swimming pool, and spa. Restaurant and cocktail lounge; meeting rooms. Handicap facilities.

Princeville Hotel. *$465-$5,000*. 5520 Ka Haku Rd., Princeville; (808) 826-9644/(800) 826-4400/*www.princeville.com*. Full-fledged, luxury resort hotel, with 252 rooms and suites, overlooking Hanalei Bay. Hotel facilities include a swimming pool, spa, health club, tennis courts, golf courses, restaurants and cocktail lounges, meeting rooms, shops and beauty salon, and an in-house cinema. Handicap facilities.

Condominiums

Ali'i Kai. *$115-$250*. 3830 Edwards Rd., Princeville; (808) 826-9775/(808) 826-7498/(800) 826-7782/*www.regencypacificrealty. com*. Oceanfront condominium complex with two-bedroom units with TV and phones. Restaurant and cocktail lounge on premises; also swimming pool, spa and health club. Golf course nearby.

Cliffs at Princeville. *$155-$400*. 3811 Edwards Rd., Princeville; (808) 826-6219/(808) 826-6585/(800) 622-6219/(800) 367-7052/ *www.cliffs-princeville.com* or *www.premierkauai.com*. 172 units with garden and ocean views; TV, phones, kitchenettes. Swimming pool, jacuzzis and sauna, putting green, recreation room and tennis courts; also meeting rooms. Handicap facilities.

Hale Makai Beach Cottages. *$195-$265*. 4400 Oneone Rd., P.O. Box 1109, Hanalei, HI 96714; (510) 841-4474/693-0062/ *www.halemakaicottages.com*. 5 one- and two-bedroom beachfront cottages located at Tunnels Beach, with TV and phones, and internet; maid service upon request. Minimum stay, 3 days.

Hale Moi. *$100-$200*. 5301 Ka Haku Rd., Princeville; (808) 826-6244/*www.vacationkauai.com*. 40 condominium units with TV and phones; most with kitchens. Suites, studios and one-bedroom units available, with mountain and garden views.

Hanalei Bay Villas. *$150-$250*. 5451 Honoiki Rd., Princeville; (808) 826-6585/(800) 222-5541/*www.oceanfrontrealty.com*. 40 one- and two-bedroom units, with TV, phones, and full kitchens.

Located on bluff overlooking Hanalei Bay.

Hanalei Colony Resort. *$180-$335.* 5-7130 Kuhio Hwy., P.O. Box 206, Hanalei, HI 96714; (808) 826-6235/(800) 628-3004/ *www.hcr.com*. Oceanfront condominium complex with 52 rental units with garden and ocean views, and kitchen facilities. Swimming pool on premises. Minimum stay, 3 days.

Hanalei House and Cottage. *$355-$795.* 5224A Weke Rd., Hanalei; (808) 338-1625/(800) 992-4632/*www.aston-hotels.com*. Six-bedroom house and adjacent one-bedroom cottage, set on 3-acre beachfront estate. Phones, TV, refrigerators. Fully-equipped kitchen on premises. Minimum stay, 7 nights.

Mauna Kai. *$115-$265.* 3970 Wyllie Rd., Hanalei, HI 96714; (808) 245-8841/(800) 367-5025/(800) 487-9833/*www.princevilleaccommodations.com* or *www.800hawaii.com*. 46 condominium units with TV and phones. Swimming pool.

Pali Ke Kua. *$175-$375.* 5300 Ka Haku Rd., Princeville; (808) 826-9066/(808) 826-9775/(800) 535-0085/(800) 826-7782/*www.marcresorts.com* or *www.regencypacificrealty.com*. 98-unit oceanfront condominium complex, offering suites and one- and two-bedroom units. TV, phones, full kitchens. Swimming pool and spa; restaurant.

Pu'u Poa. *$125-$295.* 5454 Ka Haku Rd., Princeville; (808) 826-6585/(808) 826-9602/(800) 222-5541/(800) 535-0085/*www.oceanfrontrealty.com*. Oceanfront condominium complex with 56 two-bedroom units with TV and phones. Swimming pool, tennis courts.

Sandpiper Village. *$167-$250.* 4770 Pepelani Loop, Princeville; (808) 826-9613/(808) 826-6585/(800) 222-5541/*www.oceanfrontrealty.com*. 200 condominium units, located close to Princeville golf course. Swimming pool, spa and health club on premises.

Sea Lodge. *$125-$200.* Hanalei; (800) 585-6101/(808) 826-7288/(800) 487-9833/*www.hestara.com* or *www.800hawaii.com*. 87-unit oceanfront condominium complex. TV, phones; swimming pool.

Bed and Breakfast

Hale-Aha Bed & Breakfast. *$110-$275.* 3875 Kamehameha Rd., Princeville; (808) 826-6733/(800) 826-6733. Lovely setting, on the golf course, with views of the ocean. 4 guest rooms, decorated in soft pastels; TV, refrigerators, private baths. Continental breakfast; maid service on request. Minimum stay, 3 days.

Hale Ho'o Maha Bed & Breakfast. *$150-$175.* 2495 Liliokalani St., P.O. Box 422, Kilauea, HI 96754; (808) 828-1341/(800) 851-0291/*www.aloha.net/~hoomaha*. 4 rooms with ocean and mountain views; private baths. Spacious living room, and fully-equipped kitchen for guests' use. Full breakfast with island fruit, homemade breads and granola with macadamia nuts, eggs and waffles, and local, Kauai coffee.

Hale Luana Bed & Breakfast. *$99-$125.* 4680 Kapuna Rd., Kilauea, HI 96754; (808) 828-1564. Five-bedroom, 5-bath home in tropical setting, overlooking pool, with views of ocean and mountains; also two guest bedrooms with private baths and private entrances available in adjacent house. Hawaiian decor and furnishings, spacious great room, fully-equipped kitchen, TV, VCR, stereo. Swimming pool. Full breakfast.

Dining | Kilauea, Princeville, Hanalei

[Restaurant prices—based on full course dinner, excluding drinks, tax and tips—are categorized as follows: *Deluxe*, over $30; *Expensive*, $20-$30; *Moderate*, $10-$20; *Inexpensive*, under $10.]

Bali Hai. *Moderate-Expensive.* At the Hanalei Bay Resort, 5380 Honoiki Rd., Princeville; (808) 826-6522. Splendid ocean and mountain views. Specializes in Pacific Rim cuisine, featuring fresh fish, baked salmon, barbecued Thai shrimp, filet mignon and lamb chops. Nightly entertainment; cocktails. Open for breakfast, lunch and dinner. Reservations recommended.

Cafe Hanalei. *Moderate-Expensive.* At the Princeville Hotel, 5520 Kahako Road, Princeville; (808) 826-2760. Specializing in Pacific Rim cuisine. Also offers extensive Thai and seafood buffets. Open for breakfast, lunch and dinner daily, and Sunday brunch.

Chuck's Steak House. *Moderate-Expensive.* Princeville Shopping Center, Kuhio Hwy., Princeville; (808) 826-6211. Fresh fish, lobster, prime rib and top sirloin. Also teriyaki chicken, salads, burgers and sandwiches. Informal setting. Lunch and dinner daily. Reservations recommended.

Hanalei Gourmet. *Inexpensive-Moderate.* 5-5161 Kuhio Hwy., Hanalei; (808) 826-2524. Deli-style sandwiches, served on freshly-baked breads. Also fresh fish, homemade lasagna and pasta dishes. Tropical bar; live entertainment, Tues.-Sat. Open for breakfast, lunch and dinner.

Hanalei Dolphin. *Moderate.* Hanalei; (808) 826-6113. Outdoor setting, in Polynesian atmosphere; overlooking Hanalei River. Menu features fresh fish, abalone, tenderloin steak, buffalo steak and chicken. Also cocktails. Open for dinner. Reservations suggested.

Kilauea Bakery/Pau Hana Pizza. *Moderate.* Kong Lung Center, Kilauea Road, Kilauea; (808) 828-2020. Wide selection of breads and pastries, including goat cheese and sun dried tomatoes bread and fruit-flavored Danishes and chocolate scones. Also traditional and specialty pizzas. Open for breakfast, lunch and dinner daily.

La Cascata. *Moderate-Expensive.* At the Princeville Hotel, 5520 Ka Haku Rd., Princeville; (808) 826-9644. Intimate dining room, with classic Italian decor, overlooking Hanalei Bay and Bali Hai. House specialties include oven-baked sea bass, veal scallopini, and grilled sirloin. Open for dinner; also Sunday brunch. Reservations recommended.

Pizza Hanalei. *Inexpensive.* Ching Young Village Shopping Ctr., Hanalei; (808) 826-9494. Wide selection of pizzas, with home-made whole-wheat or white-flour crust. Also lasagna, salads, and garlic bread. Lunch and dinner daily.

Tahiti Nui. *Moderate.* Kuhio Hwy., Hanalei; (808) 826-6277. American and Thai cuisine, served in Polynesian setting. Specialties include fresh island fish, chicken curry, and family-style calamari. Luaus Wednesdays and Fridays. Open for lunch and dinner daily. Reservations suggested.

NORTH SHORE | Dining

HAWAIIAN FLOWERS

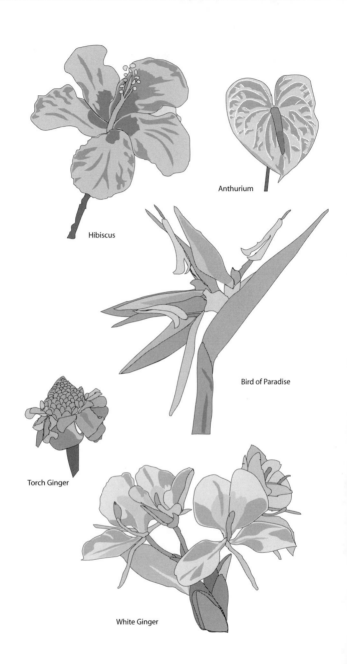

Hibiscus

Anthurium

Bird of Paradise

Torch Ginger

White Ginger

HAWAIIAN FLOWERS

Plumeria

Passion Flower

Lobster Claw

Miss Joaquin Orchids

Silversword

HAWAIIAN SEASHELLS

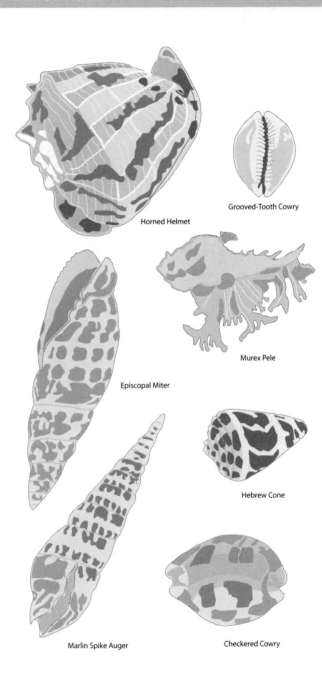

Horned Helmet

Grooved-Tooth Cowry

Murex Pele

Episcopal Miter

Hebrew Cone

Marlin Spike Auger

Checkered Cowry

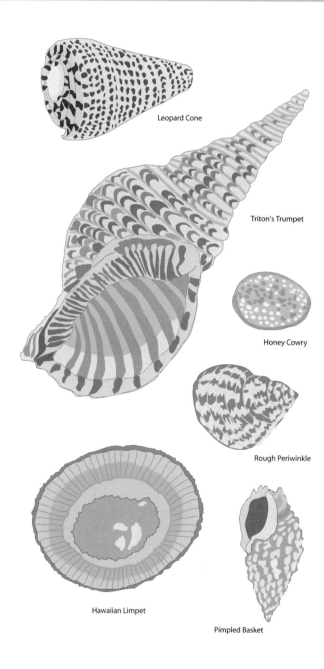

Leopard Cone

Triton's Trumpet

Honey Cowry

Rough Periwinkle

Hawaiian Limpet

Pimpled Basket

THINGS TO SEE AND DO

Places to See | **Points of Interest at a Glance**

Lihue Area

Grove Farm Homestead. Nawiliwili Rd., Lihue; (808) 245-3202. Authentic, wonderfully preserved, 80-acre plantation-era estate, originally established in 1864 by plantation owner George N. Wilcox. Comprises a main plantation home, cottages and workers' smaller camp houses. View early-day, plantation-era artifacts, including period furnishings and fixtures, and several personal items, all left more or less untouched, in their original state, reflective of a bygone era. 2-hour guided tours of estate, offered by reservation, at 10 a.m. and 1 p.m., on Mon., Wed., Thurs. Admission: $5.00 adults, $2.00 children 12 and under (tour not recommended for young children).

Kauai Museum. 4428 Rice Street, Lihue; (808) 245-6931/*www. kauaimueum.org*. Housed in historic Wilcox Memorial Library Building, dating from the 1930s. Museum features on-going video, "The Story of Kauai," depicting the history of the island, from its geological formation to present day, including the development of Kauai's society and culture. Also on display are several artifacts and exhibits of local historical interest, including such items as stone mortars and pestles from ancient Hawaiian times, sugar plantation-era tools, old photographs, and replicas of a Japanese worker's spartan quarters and a plantation owner's home, with original koa wood furnishings. Museum hours: 9-4 Mon.-Fri., 10-4 Sat. Admission fee: $7.00 adults, $5.00 seniors, $3.00 children (13-17), $1.00 children (5-12), and free admission for children under 5 years.

Kilohana Plantation. Located 1½ miles west of Lihue, on Kaumuali'i Highway (50), Puhi; (808) 245-5608/*www.kilohanakau-ai.com*. Former sugar plantation estate, dating from the 1930s, situated on 35 acres amid sugarcane fields. Beautifully restored, and furnished in part in Art Deco style. Now houses shops and art galleries, and a courtyard restaurant. Carriage rides and tours of the grounds and nearby cane fields are offered, in carriages drawn by Clydesdales. Cost for 20-minute carriage ride is $12.00 per person; admission to the plantation and walking tours are free. Open 9.30 a.m.-9.30 p.m., Mon.-Sat., and 9.30 a.m.-5 p.m. on Sundays. Also restaurant on premises, open for breakfast, lunch and dinner.

Alakoko (Menehune) Fishpond Lookout. Located on Hulemalu Road (which goes off Wa'apa Road), west of Nawiliwili Harbor. Overlooks ancient Hawaiian fishpond, with 5-foot-high and 100-foot-long stone walls, believed to have been built by Kauai's legendary people, the *menehune*, in the course of a single night. The pond is located on the Hule'ia River, locale of the *Raiders of the Lost Ark*, on private property; view from the roadside.

Hule'ia National Wildlife Refuge. Situated adjacent to the Menehune Fishpond, and also viewed from the fishpond lookout; (808) 828-1413. 241-acre wetlands preserve, established in 1973 to protect Hawaiian waterbirds. There are 31 species of endangered birds at the refuge, including the Koloa maoli (duck), moorhen, coot and the Hawaiian stilt. Closed to the public; view from the fishpond lookout.

Wailua Falls. Located approximately 5 miles north of Lihue, at the end of Ma'alo Road (583), which is off Kuhio Highway (56) just north of Lihue. Picturesque, 80-foot twin falls, quite possibly Hawaii's most photographed and most famous waterfalls, featured in the opening scenes of the TV series, *Fantasy Island*. Picnicking possibilities.

South Shore

Koloa History Center. Koloa Rd., Old Koloa Town. The museum is in fact part of the old Koloa Hotel complex, featuring a courtyard setting, with a recreated, early 1900s barber shop with antique fixtures, and samples of sugarcane, period photographs of Koloa Landing and Old Koloa Town, and several artifacts centered around local history, including such items as a rice thresher, old wooden rakes and saws, antique washing and sewing machines, and a 19th-century Japanese bath tub. Museum hours: 9 a.m.-8 p.m. daily.

Spouting Horn. Just off Lawai Rd., approximately 3 miles west of Poipu. One of Hawaii's best-known and most visited blowholes, where water gushes forth in geyser-like plumes, from a lava tube, when the pressure builds up from sea swells.

National Tropical Botanical Garden. Located at the end of Hailima Rd. (which goes south off Koloa Rd.) in Lawai; (808) 332-7361/*www.ntbg.org*. The National Tropical Botanical Garden was chartered by the U.S. Congress in 1964 and opened to the public in 1971. Its principal property here, the 252-acre *McBryde Garden*, boasts lavish displays of tropical plants from throughout the world, and is one of the world's great tropical research gardens, devoted to research and education in tropical plants. The adjacent, 100-acre *Allerton Gardens*, originally established in 1938 by Robert Allerton and his adopted son, John Gregg Allerton, also features tropical plants, including several rare South Pacific plants introduced to Kauai by the Allertons. Also at the Allerton Gardens is the preserved, former home of Queen Emma, wife of King Kamehameha IV. Guided tours of McBryde Garden are offered at 9 a.m. and 1 p.m, and tours of Allerton Garden are offered at 9 a.m, 10 a.m., 1 p.m. and 2 p.m. Tours depart from the Visitor Center across from Spouting Horn, and last approximately 2½ hours. Reservations are required and can be made at (808) 742-2623. Tour cost: $15.00 per person for McBryde Gardens; $30.00 per person for Allerton Gardens.

West Side

Koke'e Natural History Museum. Situated at the Koke'e State Park, on Koke'e Rd., 16 miles north of Waimea; (808) 335-9975/ *www.koke'e.org*. Small museum, housing exhibits of Hawaiian artifacts and indigenous wildlife; also provides interpretive, educational programs and displays centered around Kauai's geology, climate and ecology. The museum includes a book section specializing in Hawaiian interest books and maps of the area, both general and trail maps. Open 10 a.m.-4 p.m., 365 days a year. Free admission.

Russian Fort Elizabeth State Park. Off Kaumuali'i Hwy. (50), 6½ miles west of Hanapepe (22½ miles west of Lihue). 17-acre park, situated on the east bank of the Waimea River. The park has in it the ruins of a Russian fort that was originally built between 1815 and 1817; it was built for the Russians, but by a German architect, Georg Anton Scheffer, and named for Czarina Elizabeth, wife of Alexander I. A self-guided walk leads past remnants of the fort. Open during daylight hours.

Menehune Ditch. Situated on Menehune Rd. (which goes off Kaumuali'i Hwy.), 1½ miles north of Waimea. One of Kauai's architectural marvels—with its unique construction, featuring flanged and fitted cut-stone bricks, interlocking almost perfectly—attributed to the island's legendary people, the *menehune*. The original ditch was built as an aqueduct, some 24 feet high, to irrigate the *taro* patches in the valley. Only a small portion of the ditch now remains visible.

East Side

Fern Grotto. On the Wailua River, inland from Wailua. Popular tourist attraction, and setting for hundreds of weddings every year. Comprises a natural amphitheater-like cave, with huge, overhanging ferns inside it, which contribute to some unique acoustics. The Fern Grotto can be reached only by boat, upriver; musicians enliven the boat trips with Hawaiian melodies and sing-along songs along the way. Tour boats depart every half-hour, 8 a.m.-4 p.m. daily; tour cost: $20.00 adults, $10.00 children. For more information on Fern Grotto tours, contact *Smith's Motor Boat Service,* (808) 821-6892/ *www.smithskauai.com.*

Kauai Children's Discovery Museum. Housed in the Kauai Village Shopping Center, 4-831 Kuhio Hwy. (56), Waipouli; (808) 823-8222/*www.kcdm.org.* Interactive, hands-on exhibits for children, both pre-teen and teen, centered around Kauai's flora, fauna and natural history. Among the many fun and educational exhibits are a "Volcano Climb" and "Submarine Expedition." Also StarLab Planetarium, art workshops with professional artists, activity tables and Keiki Camp for children 5 to 10 years old. Open Mon.-Fri., 7.30 a.m.-5.30 p.m.

Smith's Tropical Paradise. Located at the Wailua Marina State Park, Wailua; (808) 821-6895/*www.smithskauai.com.* 30-acre cultural and botanical garden, with self-guided paths meandering through beautifully landscaped grounds, amid Kauai's exotic plants, flowers and trees. There are also replicas of Japanese, Filipino and Polynesian villages here, representative of the ethnic diversity of the people of Kauai. Garden luau and international show featured every night, showcasing the entertainment and foods of Tahiti, Hawaii, China, Japan, the Philippines, New Zealand and Samoa. Open 8.30-4 daily. Admission fee: $5.00 adults, $2.50 children; luau $65.00 adults, $30.00 children (7-13), $20.00 children (3-6).

Opaeka'a Falls. Situated approximately 2 miles west of Wailua on Kuamo'o Rd. (580), which goes off Kuhio Hwy. (50). Scenic 40-foot waterfalls. Picnicking possibilities. Large parking area nearby.

Kamokila Hawaiian Village. Situated at 6060 Kuamo'o Road (Hwy. 580), 2 miles west of Wailua; (808) 823-0559/*www. kamokila.com.* Recreated, ancient Hawaiian village, situated amid taro fields, and comprising a handful of buildings as well as exhibits. Also demonstrations of poi making and mat and skirt weaving. Open 9-5 daily. Admission: $5.00 per person. Also offered are outrigger canoe rides along the Wailua River. Cost: $30.00 adults and $20.00 children (5-12) for a 2½-hour canoe ride; $45.00 adults and $30.00 children (5-12) for a 3½-hour ride and tour of the Fern Grotto, which includes village admission.

Keahua Arboretum. Located on Kuamo'o Rd. (Hwy. 580), some 6½ miles from Kuhio Hwy., inland from Wailua. Lovely, 12-acre preserve, part of the U.S. Forest area. Features more than 20 species of plants; also picnicking, hiking, and swimming possibilities in nearby stream. A half-mile loop trail also leads to a small, natural pool, with a rope swing for swinging out over the water. Open during daylight hours.

North Shore

Kilauea Point National Wildlife Refuge. Situated at the northern end of Kilauea Rd. (which goes off Kuhio Hwy.) in Kilauea; (808) 828-1413/*www.kilaueapoint.com*. Spectacular, 203-acre coastal park, which includes in it Kilauea Point, the northernmost point on the main Hawaiian islands. The refuge is a nesting colony for endangered seabirds, including red-footed boobies, wedge-tailed shearwaters, laysan albatross and great frigate birds, all of which can be seen here, along the rugged coastline. Also, in the winter and spring months, you can see various marine life here, just off the coast, including whales, dolphins, seals and sea turtles. At Kilauea Point there is also an old lighthouse, the *Kilauea Lighthouse*, built in 1913, and still in operation. Park hours: 10-4 daily; admission: $3.00 adults, children (16 and under) free.

Guava Kai Plantation. Situated at the *mauka* (inland) end of Kuawa Road in Kilauea; (808) 828-6121/*www.guavakai.com*. 480-acre guava orchard, with guava processing plant on premises. Self-guided tours of orchards and processing plant; also guava jams, jellies, juices and other guava products available for sampling and retail sale. Hours: 9-5 daily. Free admission.

Wai'oli Mission House Museum. Located on Kuhio Hwy. (560), just west of mile marker 3, in Hanalei; (808) 245-3202. Housed in former home of missionaries Abner and Lucy Wilcox, originally built in 1837 and restored in 1921. Features original missionary furnishings from the late 1800s, including antique koa furniture, as well as the original wood-burning stove and bookcases lined with several volumes from Abner Wilcox' collection. Museum hours: 9 a.m.-3 p.m., Tues., Thurs., Sat. Donations accepted.

Ha'ena State Park. Off Kuhio Hwy. (560), approximately 7 miles west of Hanalei. 230-acre park, which includes in it *Ha'ena Beach, Ke'e Beach*, some archaeological sites, and the north shore landmarks, *Waikapalae and Waikanaloa Wet Caves*, located just inside the park, and with their associations to the Hawaiian goddess of fire, Pele. The caves, typically, are deep, dark, and large, with stagnant water. Park open during daylight hours.

Ka'ulu a Paoa Heiau. Located near the western end of Ke'e Beach (which lies in the Ha'ena State Park, off Kuhio Hwy.), and reached by way of a trail, journeying along the shoreline, past the historic Allerton House, then up the hill to the *heiau*. The ancient *heiau* is dedicated to Laka, the Hawaiian goddess of the *hula*, where she, in fact did much of her dancing. Dedicated students of the *hula* still make the pilgrimage to this most sacred shrine of the dance. The site of the *heiau* also offers good all-round views.

Places to Go | Beaches

All beaches in the Hawaiian islands are public beaches, and nude bathing at public beaches is prohibited under Hawaiian state law (even though a few of them continue to be unofficial nudist beaches). Visitors to Hawaii's beaches should also be forewarned that coastal waters are subject to strong undercurrents or rip tides, especially during winter and spring, and caution should be exercised.

Lihue Area

Hanama'ulu Beach Park. Located at Hanama'ulu Bay, at the end of Hehi Rd. (which goes off Hanama'ulu Rd., which, in turn, goes off Kuhio Hwy.), approximately 2½ miles northeast of Lihue. The beach, lined with ironwood trees, is a favorite of locals. It has a safe swimming area, especially suited to children, as well as picnicking, camping and fishing possibilities.

Kalapaki Beach. Situated along Kalapaki Bay, at the bottom of Rice St. and Wapa'a Rd., in Lihue; fronts on the Marriott Kauai resort. Popular beach, long, wide, sandy, and with gentle waves, offering safe swimming conditions. The beach is also well-liked by sailing and surfing enthusiasts.

Nukoli'i Beach Park. Situated some 3½ miles north of Lihue, bordering on the Wailua Golf Course and the Aston Kauai Beach Villas; reached by way of Kuhio Hwy. (56) north, then Kauai Beach Rd. (which goes off Hwy. 56, roughly a half mile north of the intersection of Hwys. 56 and 51), then right onto an unmarked road (½ mile from the Kauai Beach Rd. turnoff), which leads to the beach. Nukoli'i is a narrow, 2-mile-long sandy beach, popular with beachcombers, picnickers, and fishermen. Facilities include restrooms and showers; also ample parking.

South Shore

Brennecke Beach. Situated off Ho'owili Rd., a quarter mile east of Poipu Beach Park. Small, sandy beach, with a shore break with high energy waves. The beach is a good place for bodysurfing and boogie-boarding. No facilities.

Lawai Beach. Off Lawai Rd., just west of Prince Kuhio Park (which lies 1½ miles west of Poipu). Narrow, roadside beach. Offers fair swimming and snorkeling conditions, but good surfing possibilities, with generally consistent waves—the biggest occurring in the summer months—and a series of surf breaks—"Smokey's," "PK's," "Centers" and "Acid Drop." Showers and restroom facilities at beach.

Maha'ulepu. Located approximately 2½ miles northeast of Poipu; reached by way of Poipu Rd. northeastward to the end, then right onto an unmarked cane road that eventually leads to the beach. Long, sandy beach, protected by a coral reef and backed by shallow sand dunes and indigenous vegetation. The beach is quite popular with surfers, windsurfers, and fishermen. No facilities.

Shipwreck Beach. Situated at the end of Ainako Rd. (which goes off Poipu Rd.), and fronting on the Hyatt Regency in Poipu. A partly-sandy partly-coral beach, where swimming is inadvisable. Well-liked by bodysurfers, although the pounding shore break here makes the sport dangerous for amateurs.

Poipu Beach Park. Located at the end of Ho'oni Rd. (which goes off Poipu Beach Rd.), in Poipu. This crescent-shaped, sandy beach is one of the most popular in Kauai, both for swimming and snorkeling. It features several pavilions, picnic tables, and showers and restroom facilities. The beach park also incorporates in it a section known as *Baby Beach*, which has a good swimming area, protected by a reef just offshore.

Sheraton Beach (Poipu Beach). Fronting on the Sheraton Kauai and the Kiahuna Plantation Resort in Poipu; reached by way of a public access road at the end of Ho'onani Rd. (which goes off Kapili Rd., which, in turn, goes off Poipu Rd.). Also a crescent-shaped, sandy beach, with good sunbathing, swimming, surfing and windsurfing possibilities. Showers are available at the beach.

West Side

Kekaha Beach Park. Situated at Kekaha, 3 miles west of Waimea, off Kaumuali'i Hwy. (50). Secluded, white-sand beach, backed by shallow sand dunes, which marks the beginning of the 12-mile stretch of beach extending up the coast to the Polihale State Park. The beach, however, is frequented primarily by fishermen and dedicated surfers, and swimming is not advised due to the strong longshore currents and rip tides.

Lucy Wright Beach Park. Located on the western bank of the Waimea River, off Kaumuali'i Hwy. (50), at Waimea. The beach has dark sand, driftwood, and muddy water close in to the shore, due largely to its location adjacent to the mouth of the river. Beach facilities include restrooms and showers; also camping possibilities.

Majors Bay. Located approximately 7 miles northwest of Kekaha, just off Kaumuali'i Hwy. (50); beach access is generally permitted through the Pacific Missile Range facility. Long, wide, white-sand beach, also popular with fishermen and surfers; offers some of the best surfing conditions on the island. Swimming is not encouraged due to unfavorable ocean currents. No beach facilities.

Pakala Beach. Located near the village of Pakala, west of Hanapepe, and reached on Kaumuali'i Hwy. (50), and a dirt trail that goes off the highway, at mile marker 21, passing through a cane field and leading down to the beach. Pakala is a beautiful beach, with superb views of the island of Ni'ihau just offshore. The beach also has a locally-famous surf break known as "Infinities," with its exceptionally long waves, reaching heights of 8-10 feet in the summer months. No facilities.

Polihale State Park. Located roughly a mile north of Majors Bay (8 miles northwest of Kekaha), off Kaumuali'i Hwy. (50), and reached by way of a sign-posted dirt road that goes off the highway, left (or north), some 5 miles, ending at the beach. Polihale is one of Hawaii's most beautiful, secluded, white-sand beaches, 4 miles long and almost 100 yards wide at places, backed by sand dunes that are 50-100 feet high. Offers beachcombing and surfing opportunities; swimming is not advised due to the unsafe ocean conditions. Beach facilities include restrooms and showers; also some camping possibilities, by permit.

Salt Pond Beach Park. Situated just to the southwest of Hanapepe; reached by way of Lele Rd. (which goes off Kaumuali'i Hwy. (50), just past mile marker 17, west of Hanapepe), then right onto Lokokai Rd. which leads to the beach. The beach is crescent-shaped and well-liked by area residents. It is protected by a reef just offshore, and offers safe swimming conditions. Beach facilities include picnic tables, pavilions, campsites, and showers and restrooms; also on-duty lifeguard.

East Side

Anahola Beach Park. Situated on Anahola Bay, approximately 3½ miles north of Kapa'a; reached by way of Kuhio Hwy. (56) north, then northeastward onto Kukuihale Rd. at mile marker 13, and right onto a dirt access road, a mile farther, which leads to the beach. Anahola is a long, narrow beach, bordered by shady ironwood trees and protected by a reef, making it safe for swimming; during high surf conditions, however, dangerous rip tides do occur, with swimming becoming inadvisable. Beach facilities include picnic tables, showers and restrooms.

Donkey Beach. Located just over 1½ miles north of Kealia Beach (see above), and reached by way of a short walk from the latter. Picturesque, crescent-shaped sandy beach, quite popular with nudists. Swimming is not encouraged here due to the dangerous undercurrents. No facilities.

KAUAI | Beaches

Kapa'a Beach Park. Situated at the end of Niu Rd. (which goes off Kuhio Hwy.), in Kapa'a. Narrow, sandy beach; attracts primarily fishermen, as well as some dedicated swimmers.

Kealia Beach. Situated off Kuhio Hwy. (56), at mile marker 10, just north of Kapa'a. Lovely, crescent-shaped sandy beach, lying between two rocky points on the coast. Offers good surfing and bodysurfing, although swimming is unsafe due to the prevailing strong ocean currents here. For swimmers, there is a small jetty at the north end of the beach, which offers safe swimming conditions in calm weather. No beach facilities.

Larsens Beach. Northwest of Moloa'a Bay (see above); reached by way of Ko'olau Rd. southeast off Kuhio Hwy. (56) near mile marker 20, then off on a dirt road, 1¼ miles farther, which leads to the beach. Larsens is a long, narrow, sandy beach, backed by low sand dunes and shade trees. Popular activities here are beachcombing and fishing; swimming is not recommended, due to the encroaching coral. No facilities.

Lydgate State Park. Located just south of Wailua, off Kuhio Hwy. (56); reached by way of Leho Dr. (which goes off the highway, east, at mile marker 5), then Nalu Rd. to the very end. Popular family beach, with a breakwater, built from boulders, to protect the beach from a shore break. Offers safe swimming, picnicking, beachcombing and fishing possibilities. Facilities at the park include picnic tables, restrooms and showers.

Moloa'a Bay. Located approximately 7 miles north of Kapa'a, at the end of Moloa'a Rd. (which goes off Ko'olau Rd, which, in turn, goes off Kuhio Hwy. (56), just north of mile marker 16). Secluded, crescent-shaped beach, rarely visited, offering promising beachcombing and shell-collecting possibilities. Swimming is not advised during high surf, when strong undercurrents are likely to occur. No beach facilities.

Wailua Beach Park. Off Kuhio Hwy. (56), at mile marker 6, in Wailua. Well-liked area beach, half-mile long, and situated near the mouth of the Wailua River. Some swimming possibilities, with on-duty lifeguard; however, exercise caution when entering the ocean here, as strong rip currents do occur at various points along the beach, especially near the mouth of the river.

North Shore

Anini Beach Park. Off Anini Rd., which goes off the second Kalihiwai Rd., which, in turn, goes off Kuhio Hwy. (56), ½ mile west of mile marker 25, between Kilauea and Princeville. This is a very popular beach, protected from the ocean by a long, wide reef, just offshore. It offers good possibilities for snorkeling, beachcombing, windsurfing, and fishing. Facilities at the park include picnic tables and showers and restrooms.

Black Pot Beach Park. Located at the end of Weke Rd., just past the Hanalei Beach Park (see above). Black Pot is a popular area beach, long, sandy, and offering promising swimming, surfing and windsurfing possibilities. Beach facilities include picnic tables, showers and restrooms.

Ha'ena Beach Park. Off Kuhio Hwy. (56), near mile marker 9, ¼ mile west of Tunnels Beach. Offers campsites and showers and restroom facilities. Swimming is not advised due to the prevailing strong undercurrents.

Ha'ena State Park (Ke'e Beach). At the end of Kuhio Hwy. (56), at mile marker 10. Excellent swimming and snorkeling beach—in calm seas only—protected from the open ocean by a large reef; during high surf conditions, however, the strong ocean currents can often be dangerous. The beach has a lifeguard, and showers and restroom facilities.

Hanakapi'ai Beach. 2 miles southwest of Ke'e Beach, reached on the Kalalau Trail. Hanakapi'ai is a picturesque, white-sand beach in summertime; however, in the winter months, the high surf washes away the beach to expose boulders. Swimming inadvisable due to dangerous undercurrents, even in seemingly calm conditions.

Hanalei Beach Park. North of Hanalei, on Hanalei Bay; reached by way of Aku Rd. north from Hanalei town, then right onto Weke Rd. which leads to the beach. 2-mile-long beach, quite popular with families. On-duty lifeguard, and picnic tables and restroom facilities.

Kahili Beach (Quarry Beach). Located just northeast of Kilauea, and reached by way of Kilauea Rd., ¼ mile north of the Kong Lung Center, then east onto an unmarked dirt road, which leads, another 1½ miles, directly to the beach. The beach is quite popular with surfers and fishermen. Swimming is not advised in the winter and spring months, and during high surf conditions, due to the dangerous rip tides. No beach facilities.

Kalalau Beach. Situated at the mouth of the Kalalau Valley, 11 miles southwest of Ke'e Beach; accessed only by way of the rugged Kalalau Trail, or by boat. Long, sandy beach in secluded setting, with a pounding shore break; in the winter and spring months the beach gives way to exposed boulders. Dangerous rip currents, even in calm seas. Swimming not advised; approach ocean with extreme caution.

Kalihiwai Beach. Located at the end of Kalihiwai Rd. (which goes off Kuhio Hwy.), ½ mile northwest of Kilauea. Wide, sandy beach, bordered by ironwood trees, quite popular with surfers during the winter and spring months. Swimming is inadvisable due to the strong rip tides and pounding shore break. No facilities.

Kauapea Beach (Secret Beach). North of Kilauea; reached on

Kuhio Hwy. (56) west from Kilauea, approximately ½ mile, then right on Kalihiwai Rd., a little way, to a dirt road that heads out north to the beach parking area. This is a long, wide, white-sand beach, especially popular with nudists. Swimming, as with other north shore beaches, is not encouraged here during the winter and spring months, when strong undercurrents make it unsafe for the activity. No beach facilities.

Lumahai Beach. 3 miles west of Hanalei; reached by way of Kuhio Hwy. (560) west, ¾ mile past mile marker 4, then right onto a dirt trail leading down to the beach. This is one of the loveliest and most famous of Kauai's beaches, which provided the setting for the 1950s classic, *South Pacific*. The white-sand beach is ¾ mile long, with some swimming and snorkeling possibilities in the summer months, when the ocean is calm; for the most part, however, the ocean here is unsafe, with dangerous rip tides and undercurrents. The west end of the beach—where the Lumahai River drains into the ocean, and which is reached from the beach parking area, ¾ mile west of mile marker 5 on the Kuhio Hwy. (560)—is popular with experienced bodysurfers, surfers and boogie-boarders. No beach facilities.

Pu'u Poa Beach/Makua Beach. Situated at the foot of Princeville Hotel in Princeville, with a public right-of-way at the hotel leading down to the beach. The beach is long, sandy, and protected by a reef, offering good snorkeling possibilities when the ocean is calm.

Sea Lodge Beach. Situated near the Sea Lodge Condominiums in Princeville, and reached by way of Kamehameha Rd. (which goes off Kahaku Rd., the main road leading into Princeville from Kuhio Hwy.) to the very end—at the condominium complex—from where a short walk leads past the condominiums—between blocks B and C and around block A, on the ocean side—following the coastline west to the beach. The beach is part of a small, secluded cove, and offers some swimming possibilities when the ocean is calm; however, strong undercurrents do occur due to the open ocean and can frequently make the it unsafe.

Tunnels Beach. Situated off Kuhio Hwy. (560), ½ mile past mile marker 8 (2 miles west of Wainiha). There are two access trails leading down from the highway to the beach: the first, a mile west of Surf's on the Beach restaurant; and the second, two-tenths of a mile farther west from there, with a white access marker located at the turnoff. This is a very popular beach, protected by a large reef and offering a variety of activities, depending on the season and ocean conditions. Excellent diving and snorkeling possibilities during the summer months; and in the winter months, the high surf in the area attracts world-class surfers to a point beyond the reef, known as "Tunnels." The beach also offers some windsurfing when the winds are strong enough. No facilities.

Waiakalua Iki Beach and Waiakalua Nui Beach. Situated east of Kilauea, and reached by way of North Waiakalua Rd. (which goes off Kuhio Hwy.(56), ¾ mile past mile marker 20), then *makai*—toward the ocean—onto a small dirt road, to the end, from where a short, steep trail leads down to *Waiakalua Iki Beach*, a narrow, secluded beach, lined with coral and rock, but with good beachcombing possibilities. Adjoining to the west of Waiakalua Iki Beach, just around a rocky outcropping, is *Waiakalua Nui Beach*, a large, sandy beach at the foot of a deep, lush valley. Waiakalua Nui also has good beachcombing possibilities. Swimming is not encouraged at either of the beaches due to the coral and unpredictable ocean currents. No facilities.

Waikoko Beach. Located on the west side of Hanalei Bay, off Kuhio Hwy. (560), at mile marker 4. Ironwood-lined beach, with a protective reef and safe swimming area suitable for children. Also offers good snorkeling possibilities when the ocean is calm. No facilities.

Wainiha Beach Park. Situated off Kuhio Hwy. (560), near mile marker 7, in Wainiha. Wainiha means "unfriendly water," and the ocean here is indeed dangerous, with strong rip tides; swimming should not be attempted. No facilities. The beach is frequented primarily by fishermen.

Wai'oli Beach Park. On Hanalei Bay; reached on He'e Rd., which goes off Weke Rd. The beach is located at an approximate midway point on the bay, and lined with ironwoods. It offers swimming possibilities in calm seas, during the summer months; in winter and spring, the high surf, with its huge, pounding waves and accompanying rip tides and undercurrents, make it unsafe for the activity. Beach facilities includes restrooms and showers.

Best Snorkeling Beaches

Anini Beach. Located on the north shore, off Anini Rd., which goes off the second Kalihiwai Rd., which, in turn, goes off Kuhio Hwy. (56), ½ mile past mile marker 25, west of Kilauea. Popular snorkeling beach, ideal for beginners, with a protective coral reef just offshore.

Ke'e Beach. Situated at the end of Kuhio Highway (560), at mile marker 10, in the Ha'ena State Park. This is an excellent snorkeling and swimming beach, protected from the open ocean by a large coral reef, and offering a variety of marine life. Snorkeling is not recommended during high surf conditions, when the strong ocean currents can often be dangerous.

Lawai Beach. Situated off Lawai Rd., just to the west of Prince Kuhio Park, approximately 1½ miles from Poipu. Offers good snorkeling in shallow waters, over a lava bed, some 50 yards from the shore. The beach is protected by a coral reef.

Lydgate State Beach Park. Located just south of Wailua, and reached by way of Kuhio Hwy. (56) north from Lihue, then east onto Leho Dr. at mile marker 5, and off onto Nalu Rd. to the very end. Offers an excellent snorkeling area for beginners, protected by a rock wall. Popular with vacationing families.

Poipu Beach Park. Located at the end of Ho'oni Rd. (which goes off Poipu Beach Rd.), in Poipu. This is one of Kauai's most popular snorkeling beaches, crescent-shaped and with a sandy bottom, offering excellent snorkeling possibilities quite close to the shore, with a variety of marine life.

Tunnels Beach. Located one mile west of Surf's on the Beach Restaurant (west of Hanalei and Wainiha), off Kuhio Hwy. (560), and reached by way of a dirt road that goes off the highway, seaward, to the park. This is one of best places for snorkeling in Hawaii, protected by a coral reef; it offers lava tubes and cracks and crevices in the reef, with a splendid variety of marine life. Snorkeling is not recommended in the winter months or during ocean swells.

Hiking Trails

East Side Trails

Wailua Falls Trail. The trailhead is situated off Ma'alo Rd. (which goes off Kuhio Hwy. (56), 3½ miles north of Kapa'a (or 4 miles north of Lihue). Strenuous, ½-mile trail; journeys along the south side of the Wailua River to lead to a large, natural pool at the bottom of the Wailua Falls, which has some swimming possibilities.

Nounou Mountain (Sleeping Giant) Trail. There are two trails here, leading to the top of the Nounou Ridge. The first of these, the Westside Trail, begins ½ mile north of mile marker 4 on Kuamo'o Rd. (580) (4 miles inland from Wailua), off Kamalu Rd. (581), in the Wailua Homesteads, and journeys 1½ miles, to the summit; and the other, the Eastside Trail, starts out from Haleilio Rd. (which goes off Kuhio Hwy. 56), just over a mile west from Wailua, then climbs steeply, approximately 2 miles, to the summit. The summit (elevation 1,160 ft.) has good all-round views, and picnicking possibilities.

Keahua Arboretum Trail. The trailhead is located on the south side of Kuamo'o Rd. (580), just across the stream from the Keahua Arboretum—which, in turn, is located some 7 miles west from Wailua, on Kuamo'o Rd. (which goes off Kuhio Hwy. 56). Easy, ½-mile trail, passing through an area featuring native and introduced tropical plants; there is also a natural pool here, ideal for swimming, roughly 100 yards downstream.

Kuilau Ridge Trail. The trailhead is situated on the north side of Kuamo'o Rd (580), just before reaching Keahua Arboretum (see Keahua Arboretum Trail). Scenic, 2-mile trail, with superb views of the Makaleha Mountains to be enjoyed enroute.

Moalepe Trail. This is also a scenic trail that begins near the intersection of Olohena Rd. (581)—which goes off Kuhio Hwy. (56)—and Waipouli Rd., some 3 miles west from Kapa'a. 2½-mile trail; offers views of the Makaleha Mountains and the ocean farther west.

Na Pali Coast Trails

Kalalau Trail. Begins at Ke'e Beach, at the end of Kuhio Hwy. (560), some 8 miles west of Hanalei. This is one of Kauai's most famous trails, journeying along the rugged and stunning Na Pali Coast, treating hikers to some of the most spectacular coastal scenery along the way. The trail passes by the Hanakapi'ai Beach and Hanakoa Valley and ends at the Kalalau beach and valley. Strenuous, 11-mile hike; allow at least 6 hours each way.

Hanakapi'ai Falls Trail. The trail begins at Hanakapi'ai Stream—reached on the Kalalau Trail, 2 miles southwest of Ke'e Beach—and leads inland, following the stream, to the Hanakapi'ai Falls in the Hanakapi'ai Valley. The trail also passes by some ancient stone walls, the ruins of a coffee mill, and a series of waterfalls and natural pools. 1¾ miles each way.

Hanakoa Falls Trail. Also goes off the Kalalau Trail, just west of mile marker 6, and follows the Hanakoa Stream into the Hanakoa Valley and the spectacular, 1,000-foot Hanakoa Falls, cascading into a large pool. ½-mile trail, of moderate difficulty.

Waimea Canyon and Koke'e State Park Trails

Iliau Nature Loop Trail. Easy, ½-mile loop trail, begins just before mile marker 9, off Koke'e Rd. (550). The trail winds past rare iliau plants, all clearly marked, and vista points with views of the Waimea Canyon.

Kukui Trail. Begins at the Iliau Nature Loop Trail trailhead—just south of mile marker 9 on Koke'e Rd. The trail descends some 2,000 feet to the canyon floor and the Waimea River, passing through groves of kukui nut trees along the way. 2½-mile trail.

Koaie Canyon Trail. This trail goes off the Kukui Trail (see above), and journeys alongside the Koaie Stream, on the south side, passing by several natural pools enroute, ideal for swimming. 3-mile trail;

should not be attempted when the Waimea River is high.

Canyon Trail. Strenuous, 1½-mile trail. Begins along Halemanu Rd., which goes off Koke'e Rd., just north of mile marker 14. Leads to the Waipo'o Falls and the Kumuwela Lookout which offers some of the best views of the Waimea Canyon.

Black Pipe Trail. Short, ½-mile trail, connecting the Canyon Trail (see above) to Halemanu Road.

Halemanu-Koke'e Trail. This trail also begins along Halemanu Rd., which goes off the main road, Koke'e Rd., just north of mile marker 14. The trail offers a self-guided nature walk through koa and lehua forests, abundant in native birds. 1½-mile trail.

Nature Trail. Short loop-trail, passing through small forest area, beginning and ending at the *Koke'e Natural History Museum* on Koke'e Road.

Ditch Trail. The trailhead can be reached on either Kumuwela Rd. or Mohihi Rd., roughly 1½ miles from the Koke'e State Park Headquarters. Difficult, 3½-mile trail, threading in and out of gulches; superb views enroute, of the inner canyon and its many waterfalls.

Pu'u Ka Ohelo-Berry Flat Trails. Easy, 2-mile loop-trail, which begins just off Mohihi Rd., 1½ miles from park headquarters, and winds through forests of California redwoods, Australian eucalyptus and native koa trees.

Nualolo Trail. The trail begins just west of the park headquarters, off Koke'e Rd. (550), and leads through high-altitude forests, before descending some 1,500 feet to a lookout at an elevation of 2,200 feet, directly above Nualolo Valley, which has commanding views of the Na Pali Coast. Strenuous, 4-mile trail.

Nualolo Cliff Trail. A 2-mile trail of moderate difficulty, connecting the Nualolo and Awa'awapuhi trails. Offers scenic views of the Nualolo Valley.

Awa'awapuhi Trail. One of Koke'e State Park's most popular trails; begins near mile marker 17 on Koke'e Rd. (550), and descends some 1,500 feet to an overlook (elevation 2,500 ft.) with spectacular views of the Awa'awapuhi Valley and Na Pali Coast. 3½-mile trail.

Kaluapuhi Trail. 2-mile forest trail, beginning ½ mile northeast of mile marker 17 on Koke'e Rd. (550). The trail is especially popular in the summer months, when the wild plums—to be found enroute—ripen.

Pihea Trail. The trail begins at the end of Koke'e Rd. (550), at the Pu'u o Kila Lookout, then proceeds along the rim of the Kalalau Valley for about a mile, to Pihea Peak, before descending into the Alakai Swamp, where it intersects both the Alakai Swamp and Kawaikoi Stream trails. 3¾-mile trail, of moderate difficulty.

Alakai Swamp Trail. Strenuous, 3½-mile trail, begins on Mohihi Rd.—a dirt road which may be impassable during heavy rains—near the park headquarters, and leads through Hawaii's largest swamp, containing native rain forests and bogs, ending at the Kilohana Lookout which offers good views of the Wainiha Valley and the Hanalei Bay in the distance.

Kawaikoi Stream Trail. The trailhead is located approximately midway between Kawaikoi Camp and Sugi Grove, along Mohihi Rd.—which goes off Koke'e Rd. and which may be impassable in rainy weather. Easy, 3-mile loop-trail; journeys along the Kawaikoi Stream—with several natural pools to be encountered along the way, ideal for swimming—and also passes through some beautiful forest areas.

Campgrounds

State Park Campgrounds

[For camping permits and information on state park campgrounds, contact the *Department of Land and Natural Resources*, State Office Building, 3060 Eiwa St., Room 306, Lihue, HI 96766; 808-274-3444.]

Hanakapi'ai Valley. Located 2 miles southwest of Ke'e Beach (which is 8 miles west of Hanalei, at the end of Kuhio Hwy. 560), along the Kalalau Trail. Nearby beach and waterfalls, and several little pools, ideal for swimming.

Hanakoa Valley. Situated high above the ocean, some 4 miles west of the Hanakapi'ai Valley, on the way to the Kalalau Valley. Idyllic campsites, but with the discomfort of excessive humidity and swarms of mosquitoes, frequently making the conditions unbearable.

Kalalau Valley. Situated approximately 11 miles southwest of Ke'e Beach (which is 8 miles west of Hanalei), at the end of the Kalalau Trail. There are campsites both at the Kalalau Beach and in the valley just inland. Nearby waterfalls, caves, and the broad Kalalau Valley, all well worth exploring. 5-night limit.

Koke'e State Park. Located on the west side of the island; reached by way of Kaumuali'i Hwy. (50) west to Waimea, then Waimea Canyon Rd. and Koke'e Rd. approximately 20 miles northward to the state park. The park as three campgrounds: *Kakalohui Ulhulu Meadow* (located near Koke'e Lodge), which has campsites with grills, and restrooms; *Sugi Grove* (situated off Mohihi Rd., which goes east off Koke'e Rd., 3 or 4 miles, toward Alakai Swamp), with undeveloped campsites, picnic tables and portable toilets; and *Camp 10* (2 miles past Sugi Grove), which has primarily wilderness campsites, with some picnic tables.

Miloli'i. Remote valley near the western end of the Na Pali Coast, accessible only by small boat in calm seas. Offers some wilderness campsites. Maximum stay, 3 nights.

Polihale State Park. Located on the west side of the island; reached on Kaumuali'i Hwy. (50), some 8 miles northwest from Kekaha, then 5 miles farther northwestward on a sign-posted cane road. The campsites are situated amid small sand dunes; also picnic tables, showers and restroom facilities. Maximum stay, 5 nights.

County Park Campgrounds

[For camping permits and information on county park campgrounds, contact the *County of Kauai, Division of Parks and Recreation*, 4280-A Building B, Lihue, HI 96766; 808-245-1881.]

Anahola Beach Park. Situated approximately 5 miles north of Kapa'a, near the northeast end of the island, on Anahola Bay, and reached on Kuhio Hwy. (56) and Kukuihale Rd. (which goes off the highway at mile marker 13). The campsites are located on the beach backed by ironwood trees. Facilities include showers and restrooms.

Anini Beach Park. On Kauai's north shore, between Princeville and Kilauea. Campsites are situated on Anini Beach, which has a protective reef just offshore, and offers safe swimming as well as good windsurfing possibilities. Pavilions, picnic tables, barbecue grills, showers and restrooms.

Ha'ena Beach Park. Popular camping area, located on the beach on the north shore, at Ha'ena, some 6½ miles west of Hanalei, off Kuhio Hwy. (560). Offers abundant beach activities, and pavilions, grills, showers and restrooms; swimming not advised.

Hanama'ulu Beach Park. Situated at the head of Hanama'ulu Bay, north of Lihue; reached by way of Hanama'ulu Rd. east off Kuhio Hwy. (56), ¼ mile, then east again on Hehi Rd., ½ mile, to the beach. Campsites located on beach; facilities include pavilions, picnic tables, barbecue grill, showers and restrooms. Good swimming possibilities.

Lucy Wright Park. On the west bank of Waimea River, just off Kaumuali'i Hwy. (50), in Waimea. Campsites located near the beach. Restrooms.

Niumalu Beach Park. Located near Nawiliwili Harbor in Lihue, at Wapa'a and Hulemalu Rds. Grassy camping area, with pavilions, picnic tables, grills, showers and restrooms.

Salt Pond Beach Park. Situated on Kauai's west side, just to the southwest of Hanapepe, reached by way of Kaumuali'i Hwy. (50) and Lele Rd. Well-liked campsites, located on grassy area on beach. Picnic tables, showers and restroom facilities. Also good swimming possibilities.

KAUAI | Tours and Activities

Tours and Activities

Helicopter Tours

Helicopter tours are especially popular on Kauai—perhaps more than on any other Hawaiian island—with several different companies offering flights over the Waimea Canyon, Na Pali Coast and other parts of the island. Tours originate at either the Lihue Airport in Lihue, the Port Allen Airport at Hanapepe or the Princeville Airport in Princeville, and tour companies generally utilize any of three different types of helicopters—the *Aero-Star*, a 6-seater, with all seats by the windows, offering all passengers good views; the *Hughes 500*, a 4-seater that also offers window seating to all passengers; and the *Bell Jet Ranger*, another 4-seater that has only three window seats, with one passenger being confined to a center seat and, consequently, lesser views. Tours last anywhere from 30 minutes to 90 minutes, and cost $110-$280 per person. For reservations and more information, contact any of the following:

Air Kauai. Lihue Airport, 3651 Ahukini Rd., Lihue, (808) 246-4666/(800) 972-4666/*www.airkauai.com*. Offers aerial tours of Kauai's foremost sights in its 6-passenger, air-conditioned A-Star helicopters, with Bose stereo headsets for all passengers. Tours include the Na Pali Coast, Waimea Canyon, several waterfalls, including Manawaiopuna Falls (of *Jurassic Park* fame), and the Wai'ale'ale Crater. Cost: $250.00 per person.

Blue Hawaiian Helicopters. 105 Kahului Heliport, Kahului (Maui); (808) 871-8844/(800) 745-2583/*www.bluehawaiian.com*. Aerial tours in the roomy, state-of-the-art EC130-84 ECO-Stars as well as the A-Star touring helicopters. Operates from Maui, Kauai and the Big Island, offering tours of all three islands. On Kauai, eco-adventure tours are usually 50 minutes long, and take in Hanapepe Valley, Jurassic Park Falls, Waimea Canyon, Na Pali Coast, Bali Hai, Hanalei Bay and Mt. Wai'ale'ale. Also custom-designed, all-day tours. Prices range from $230.00 per person for the Eco-Adventure Tour to $1,640.00 per hour for a private charter.

Heli USA Airways. 5-3541 Kuhio Hwy., Princeville Airport, Princeville; (808) 826-6591/*www.heliusa.com*. Variety of narrated aerial tours offered on board A-Star helicopters, including the 30-minute Kauai Highlights Island Tour that takes in Na Pali, Hanalei, Waimea Canyon, Bali Hai, and beaches and waterfalls. Also 50- to 60-minute Deluxe and Circle Island tours that include a descent into the Wai'ale'ale Crater and also include Manawaiopuna Falls. Cost: $109.00 per person for the 30-minute Island Highlights tour; $169.00 for the 50-minute Deluxe Island tour; and $199.00 for the 1-hour Circle Island tour.

Inter-Island Helicopters. 4510 Hana Rd., Hanapepe; (808) 335-

5009/(800) 656-5009/*www.interislandhelicopters.com*. Offers 50-
to 55-minute tours of the island's attractions: the Waimea Canyon
and Koke'e State Park, Na Pali Coast, Ke'e and Lumahai beaches,
Hanalei Valley and Princeville, and a descent into the Wai'ale'ale
crater. Also offers 2-hour "Waterfall Adventure Tours," which
include a waterfall landing and picnic lunch at a remote freshwater
lagoon. Cost: $189.00 for the 55-minute island tour; $300.00 for
the Waterfall Adventure Tour.

Island Helicopters. Lihue Airport, Ahukini Rd., Lihue, (808) 245-
8588/(800) 829-5999/*www.islandhelicopters.com*. Deluxe "Kauai
Grand" tour of the island in 6-seater American Eurocopter A-Stars.
Tours last 55-60 minutes, and include all the highlights of the aerial
experience: Waimea Canyon, Mt. Wai'ale'ale, Na Pali Coast, all the
famous and hidden waterfalls, valleys, bays, beaches. Cost; $250.00
per person. Attractive online discount available.

Jack Harter Helicopters. Lihue Airport, 4231 Ahukini Rd.,
Lihue, (808) 245-3774/(888) 245-2001/*www.helicopters-kauai.com*.
Fully-narrated, 60- to 90-minute island tours in 6-seater Eurocopter
A-Star helicopters. Takes in all of the island's major, scenic must-see
sights, including the stunning Na Pali Coast, Waimea Canyon and
the Wai'ale'ale crater, and the Manawaiopuna Falls in Hanapepe
Valley. Tour cost: 60-minute tour, $209.00 per person, and 90-min-
ute tour, $289.00 per person. Internet discounts available.

Ni'ihau Helicopters. Waimea; (808) 335-3500/(877) 441-3500/
www.hawaiian.net/~niihauisland/heli.html. Offers half-day helicopter tours of the "Forbidden Island," Ni'ihau. Tours include aerial
sightseeing over the island, landing on the island at a secluded
beach, with time for beachcombing, swimming and snorkeling.
Lunch, snacks and beverages are also included. Cost: $325.00 per
person.

Safari Helicopter Tours. 3225 Akahi St., Lihue; (808) 246-
0136/(800) 326-3356/*www.safarihelicopters.com*. Offers a "Deluxe
Waterfall Safari" aerial tour, with close-ups of Hanapepe Valley's
Manawaiopuna Falls (Jurassic Park Falls), scores of waterfalls
along the Na Pali Coast, and 3,000-foot falls in the rain-soaked
Wai'ale'ale Crater. Tours last 55 to 60 minutes. Cost: $209.00 per
person. Online reservations discount.

Will Squyres Helicopters. 3-3222 Kuhio Hwy., Lihue, (808) 245-
7541/(888) 245-4354/*www.helicopters-hawaii.com*. Aerial sightseeing from the air-conditioned luxury of American Eurocopter A-Star
350 helicopters. Tours take in all the stunning sights of island: Na
Pali, Wai'ale'ale, Waimea Canyon, Wailua Falls, Jurassic Park Falls,
and other landmarks. 1-hour flights, $209.00 per person; private
charters, $1,200.00 per hour.

Plane and Glider Tours

Air Ventures Hawaii. Lihue Airport, Lihue; (808) 651-0679/ *www.airventureshawaii.com*. One-hour Kauai air tours on board a high-wing, MXT7 STOL aircraft, taking in the entire island: Na Pali Coast, Waimea Canyon, Menehune Fishpond, Hanalei Valley, Hule'ia Wildlife Refuge, east side beaches, myriad waterfalls, and Wai'ale'ale. Also 30-minute tours of the eastern part of the island or the west side, with the Kilohana and Wai'ale'ale craters included on both tours. Cost: $59.00 per person for the 30-minute tour, and $99.00 per person for the 1-hour tour.

Tropical Biplanes. Lihue; (808) 246-9123/*www.tropicalbiplanes. com*. Offers 45-minute to one-hour flights over the island, on board a Waco Biplane. The one-hour ride takes in the entire island, including Poipu, Waimea Canyon, Na Pali Coast, Hanalei, Bali Hai, the East Side and Wai'ale'ale; the 45-minute tour covers about half the island. The planes are designed for two passengers, and pricing is also for two. $267.00 for two persons for a 45-minute ride; $356.00 for two persons for an hour-long flight.

Wings Over Kauai. Lihue; (808) 635-0815/*www.wingsoverkauai.com*. Offers aerial sightseeing from a high-wing Cessna 172 Skyhawk with wrap-around windows for 360° views. Tours range from 30 to 70 minutes, and take in all the premier attractions of the island, including the Na Pali Coast, Waimea Canyon, Wailua Falls, Hanapepe Valley, Anahola Ridge, Hanalei and Princeville. Cost of tours ranges from $86.00 for a 30-minute flight to $109.00 for a 65-minute flight and $125.00 for 70-minute deluxe tour.

Sightseeing Tours

Aloha Kauai Tours. 1702 Haleukana, Lihue; (808) 245-6400/(800) 452 1113/*www.alohakauaitours.com*. Offers guided four-wheel-drive tours through Waimea Canyon, Koke'e State Park, Na Pali Reserve, and the Grove Farm Homestead. Tours last 4 to 7 hours, and are conducted by knowledgeable local residents. Cost of tours: $65-$125 adults, $50-$90 children (12 and under).

Gay & Robinson Tours. 2 Kaumakani Ave., Kaumakani; (808) 335-2824/*www.gandrtours-kauai.com*. The owners offer 2-hour tours of their historic (Makaweli) sugar plantation, both of the factory and cane fields; also included are visits to the Gay & Robinson Sugar Plantation Visitor Center and Museum. 4-hour tours of the plantation on ATVs are also offered, which include lunch and some swimming. Tour cost: 2-hour plantation tour, $30.00 per person; 4-hour ATV tour, $139.00 per person.

Hawaii Movie Tours. 4885 Kuhio Hwy., Kapa'a; (808) 822-1192/(800) 628-8432/*www.hawaiimovietour.com*. Guided, "See-Kauai-Thru-Hollywood's-Eyes" tours of all of Kauai's movie locales, including *Blue Hawaii, Raiders of the Lost Ark, Jurassic Park, South Pacific, Gilligan's Island* and *Fantasy Island*. There is also a 4X4 version of the standard movie tour. Cost: $101.00 adults, $82.00 children (11 and under); 4X4 tour, $113.00 adults, $103.00 children.

Polynesian Adventure Tours. 3313-B Oihana St., Lihue; (808) 246-0122/*www.polyad.com*. Half-day and full-day tours of the Waimea Canyon, Spouting Horn, Wailua River and Fern Grotto. Tour costs: $45-$50 for the half-day tour; $67-$72 for the full-day tour.

Robert's Hawaii. 3-4567 Kuhio Hwy., Lihue Airport; (808) 539-9400/(800) 831-5541/*www.roberts-hawaii.com*. Offers narrated tours of the Waimea Canyon—which includes Old Koloa Town, Hanapepe Valley, Waimea, Old Russian Fort, Spouting Horn, and Waimea Canyon—and riverboat tours up the Wailua River to the Fern Grotto; also tours taking in both the Waimea Canyon and Fern Grotto. Tour cost: for either the Fern Grotto or Waimea Canyon tour, $45.00 adults and $32.00 children; for the combined tour, $65.00 adults and $49.00 children.

Bicycling Tours

Kauai Cycle & Tour. 1379 Kuhio Hwy., Kapa'a; (808) 821-2115. Offers bike rentals, sales and service. Rentals from $20.00 per day for a front suspension to $35.00 per day for a full suspension. Also offers information and directions to good bike trails on the island.

Island Adventures. P.O. Box 3370, Lihue, HI 96766; (808) 246-6333/*www.kauaifun.com*. Combination biking and hiking tour, which begins with a guided bicycling tour of the Kauai Lagoons resort area, then a ½-mile hike through a lush jungle area to a 50-foot waterfall. Includes bikes and helmets, and a gourmet deli lunch. Cost: $79.00 adults, $69.00 children (8-12).

Kayak Kauai. 5070-A Kuhio Hwy., Hanalei; (808) 826-9844/(800) 437-3507/*www.kayakkauai.com*. Mountain bike and beach cruiser rentals. Cost: $20.00 per day for a mountain bike, $80.00 per week; $15.00 per day for a beach cruiser, $60.00 per week. Rental includes helmet and car rack.

Outfitters Kauai. 2827A Poipu Rd. (at Poipu Plaza), Poipu Beach; (808) 742-7421/742-9667/*www.outfitterskauai.com*. Offers mountain bike and beach cruiser rentals. Also offers a 12-mile Waimea Canyon downhill bicycle tour, both in the morning and afternoon; includes all the gear, sightseeing along the way, and snacks and beverages. Cost: downhill tour, $90.00 adults, $70.00 children (12-14); bike and cruiser rentals, $20.00 per day.

Horseback Rides and Tours

CJM Country Stables. P.O. Box 1346, Koloa, HI 96756; (808) 742-6096/*wwwcjmstables.com*. Scenic coastal rides through the south shore's Maha'ulepu area, ranging from two to three hours. Cost: 2-hour ride, $90.00; 3-hour ride, $105.00.

Esprit de Corps Riding Stables. 1491 Kualapa Pl., Kapa'a; (808) 822-4688/*www.kauaihorses.com*. Variety of eco-tour trail rides in tropical mountain forest, ranging from 2 hour to all-day rides. Also beginner and English Western riding lessons and day camps. Cost: $110-$350 for trail rides; $35-$210 for riding lessons.

Princeville Ranch Stables. P.O. Box 888, Hanalei, HI 96714; (808) 826-6777/*www.princevilleranch.com*. 2,500-acre working cattle ranch, offering 1½- to 4-hour trail rides to a nearby waterfall or to ocean bluffs near Anini Beach; also ranch rides, moving cattle. Cost: 1½-hour ocean bluff ride, $65.00; 3- to 4-hour waterfall rides, $110-$120; 1½-hour cattle drive, $120.00.

Silver Falls Ranch. 2888 Kamo'okoa Rd., Kalihiwai Ridge, Kilauea; (808) 828-6718/*www.silverfallsranch.com*. 1½- to 3-hour trail rides along scenic Kamo'okoa and Kalihiwai ridges or to a waterfall, with a Hawaiian picnic lunch. Cost: ridge trail ride, $80.00; waterfall ride, $100-$120.

Boat Tours and Snorkeling Excursions

Blue Dolphin Charters. P.O. Box 869, Ele'ele, HI 96705; (808) 335-5553/(877) 511-1311/*www.kauaiboats.com*. Offers ocean tours on board its 63-foot and 65-foot catamarans, of the Na Pali Coast and the island of Ni'ihau, and sunset sails along the south shore near Poipu Beach. Includes snorkeling stops on its morning excursions; also scuba diving, fishing, and whale watching in season. Tours range from 2 hours to 7 hours. Cost: Poipu Sunset Sail, $62.54 adults ($42.40 children); Na Pali Snorkel/Scuba Tour, $126.14 adults ($83.74 children); Ni'ihau and Na Pali Snorkel/Scuba Tour, $174.90 adults ($164.30 children).

Captain Andy's Sailing Adventures. 4353 Waialo Rd., Ste. 1A-2A, Ele'ele; (808) 335-6833/(800) 535-0830/*www.capt-andys.com*

or *www.napali.com*. 2- to 5½-hour sailboat excursions aboard a 46-foot catamaran; also half-day whale-watching (Dec.-Apr.) and snorkeling excursions along the Na Pali Coast, and sunset cruises along the Na Pali Coast and the south shore near Poipu, with complimentary pupus and refreshments. Tour cost: Na Pali Snorkeling Excursion, $129.00 adults, $89.00 children; Na Pali Sunset/Dinner Cruise, $94.00 adults, $70.00 children; Poipu Sunset Cruise, $59.00 adults, $40.00 children.

Captain Sundown's Catamaran Sailing. Hanalei; (808) 826-5585/*www.captainsundown.com*. 3- and 6-hour sailing excursions to the Na Pali Coast on board a 40-foot Hawaiian-style catamaran, Afternoon tours are sightseeing trips, and morning sails include snorkeling, fishing and a deli lunch. Tour cost: 6-hour morning tour, $148.00 adults, $125.00 children; 3-hour afternoon tour, $120.00 adults, $99.00 children.

Captain Zodiac Rafting Expeditions. (Combines with Captain Andy's Sailing Adventures, with same contact information.) (808) 335-6833/(800) 535-0830/*www.napali.com*. 5- to 6-hour rafting expeditions along the Na Pali Coast, including exploration of sea caves and landing on a remote beach. Cost: 6-hour Na Pali Day Expedition, $159.00 adults, $109 children; 5-hour Na Pali Snorkeling and Picnic Excursion, $129.00 adults, $89.00 children.

Catamaran Kahanu. Hanapepe; (808) 645-6176/(888) 213-7711/*www.catamarankahanu.com*. 3½- to 5-hour excursions along the Na Pali Coast on board a 40-foot catamaran, departing from Port Allen, with some snorkeling and a hearty, Hawaiian-style buffet included. Takes in waterfalls and sea caves. Also whale watches in season. Cost: 5-hour tour, $115.00 adults, $75.00 children; 4-hour tour, $85.00 adults, $65.00 children.

Na Pali Explorer. Kikiaola Small Boat Harbor, Waimea; (808) 338-9999/(877) 335-9909/*www.napali-explorer.com*. 3- to 5-hour sightseeing boat tours of Na Pali coastline, on board a 26-foot Zodiac raft or a 48-foot power boat. Also snorkeling tours, and whale watches in season. Snacks and beverages included on sightseeing trips, and continental breakfast and deli picnic lunch on snorkeling excursions. Cost: Na Pali Sightseeing Tour, $79.00 adults, $59.00 children; Na Pali Snorkeling Tour, $125.00 adults, $85.00 children.

Na Pali Coast Hanalei. P.O. Box 9, Hanalei, HI 96714; (808) 826-6114/*www.napalitours.com*. Offers sightseeing tours along the Na Pali Coast on a 13-passenger, high-speed power boat. Also whale watches in season. Cost: $135.00 per person.

Holoholo Charters. 4469 Waialo Rd., Ele'ele; (808) 335-0815/(800) 848-6130/*www.holoholocharters.com* or *www.sail-kauai.com*. 3- to 7-hour snorkeling, sightseeing and whale-watching tours along the Na Pali Coast and the island of Ni'ihau, on board a 65-foot high-speed power catamaran, a 48-foot sailing catamaran or a 42-foot mono hull vessel. Offers morning, afternoon and sunset tours. Cost: 3½-hour sunset tour (on power catamaran), $89.00

adults, $70.00 children; 5-hour Na Pali Coast sail, $109.00 adults, $85.00 children; 7-hour Na Pali-Ni'ihau Supertour, $169.00 adults, $119.00 children.

Kauai Sea Tours. 4310 Waialo Rd., Ele'ele; (808) 826-7254/(800) 733-7997/*www.kauaiseatours.com*. Tours of the Na Pali Coast on board power catamarans or Zodiac rafts, exploring sea caves and an ancient Hawaiian fishing village, Nu'alolo Kai, and landing on secluded beaches. Scuba diving and snorkeling included on some tours, with continental breakfast and gourmet lunch. Also sunset dinner cruises, and whale watching in season. Tour cost: 4-hour sunset dinner cruise, $99.00 adults, $79.00 children; half-day tour, $129.00 adults, $99.00 children; half-day raft tour, $115.00 adults, $85.00 children; 6-hour raft tour, $132.00 adults, $102 children; 6-hour catamaran tour, $144.00 adults, $114.00 children.

Sea Fun Kauai. 1702 Haleukana St., Lihue; (808) 245-6400/(800) 452-1113/*www.alohakauaitours.com*. Offers half-day shore-based snorkeling tours inside protective reefs. Includes snorkeling gear and instruction; also lunch and beverages. Cost: $75.00 adults, $62.50 children.

Smith's Motor Boat Service. Wailua Marina State Park, Wailua; (808) 821-6892/*www.smithskauai.com*. Narrated, 1-hour 20-minute motorboat trips up the Wailua River to the Fern Grotto, with Hawaiian music on board. Tours departs every half hour, daily 9 a.m.-3.30 p.m. Cost: $20.00 adults, $10.00 children.

Scuba Diving

Scuba diving is a popular recreational sport on Kauai, with several different companies offering introductory scuba dives as well as tank dives for certified divers. Dives are offered both from the shore and from boats. Rates range from $80-$100 for introductory dives, to $65-$240 for tank dives; equipment is generally included. For more information or to schedule dives, contact any of the following dive shops:

Blue Dolphin/Ocean Odyssey Dive Shop. P. O. Box 869, Ele'ele, HI 96705; (808) 742-6731/(877) 511-1311/*www.kauai-boats.com*.

Dive Kauai Scuba Center. 1038 Kuhio Hwy., Kapa'a; (808) 822-0452/(800) 828-3483/*www.divekauai.com*.

Fathom Five Divers. 3450 Poipu Rd., P.O. Box 907, Koloa, HI 96756; (808) 742-6991/(800) 972-3078/*www.fathomfive.com*.

Mana Divers. 4310 Waialo Rd. Bay 3, Port Allen (P.O. Box 500, Ele'ele, HI 96705); (808) 742-9849/335-0881/(877) 348-3669/ *www.manadivers.com*.

Sea Sport Divers. 2827 Poipu Rd., Koloa; (808) 742-9303/(800) 685-5889/*www.seasportdivers.com*. Also has a second location: 4-976 Kuhio Hwy., Kapa'a; (808) 823-9222.

Sunrise Scuba. 1038 Kuhio Hwy., Kapa'a; (808) 822-7333?(800) 695-3483/*www.sunrisescuba.com*.

Sportfishing

Anini Fishing Charters and Tours. Kilauea; (808) 828-1285/ *www.kauaifishing.com*. Shared boat and private charters, with a maximum of 6 passengers. Deep-sea fishing and trolling; target catch: marlin, ahi, mahi mahi, ono, snapper. Cost: 4-hour share boat, $125.00 per person; 4-hour private charter, $675-$900; 6-hour private charter, $850-$1,000.

Hana Pa'a Sportfishing Charters. 6370 Kalama Rd., Kapa'a; (808) 823-6031/(866) 776-3474/*www.fishkauai.com*. Shared or private sportfishing trips on board a full-equipped 38-foot Bertram. Deep-sea fishing and trolling for marlin, tuna, mahi mahi, ono and spearfish. Cost: shared boat, $200-$300; private charter, $575-$975.

Fish Maui. (808) 879-3789/*www.fishmaui.com*. Sportfishing referrals for charter boats. Also information and advice on shore and reef fishing on Maui.

Sea Lure Charters. (808) 822-5963. Half-day and full-day sport-fishing charters, both on a share boat basis and private charters. 6-passenger maximum. Cost: Half-day shared boat, $115.00 per person; private charters, $550-$800.

Sportfish Hawaii. 575 Cooke St., #A3315, Honolulu, HI 96813; (877) 388-1376/*www.sportfishhawaii.com*. Sportfishing guide and store, arranging charters and making referrals for sportfishing trips in the islands, including Maui. Also offers charts and maps of fishing grounds, and information on sportfishing related events and tournaments.

Kayaking

Island Adventures. Nawiliwili Small Boat Harbor, P.O. Box 3370, Lihue, HI 96766; (808) 246-6333/*www.kauaifun.com*. 2¾- to 4½-hour guided kayak tours of the Hule'ia River National Wildlife Refuge and *menehune* fishpond, including visits to movie locales. Cost: 2¾-hour tour, $59.00 adults and $49.00 children; 4½-hour tour, $89.00 adults and $69.00 children.

Kayak Kauai. 5070-A Kuhio Hwy., Hanalei; (808) 826-9844/(800) 437-3507/*www.kayakkauai.com*. Offers kayak rentals as well as ½-day to 7-day organized kayak tours, including a Hanalei Bay paddle, Wailua River paddle, a full-day sea kayak tour along the south shore (from Poipu westward), as well as a full-day sea kayak tour of the Na Pali Coast, exploring remote beaches and sea caves and journeying close to towering sea cliffs. Cost of tours: 3-hour Hanalei Bay paddle, $60.00; 5-hour Wailua River paddle, $85.00 per person; Poipu sea kayak tour, $145.00; Na Pali Coast sea kayak tour, $185.00 per person (including lunch); and kayak rentals, $28-$75 per day.

Kauai Waterski. Surf and Kayak Company. 4-356 Kuhio Hwy., Kapa'a, HI 96746; (808) 822-3574/*www.kauaiwaterskisurfand-kayak.com*. Offers 4-hour guided kayak tours up the Wailua River to Ulu'wehe Falls, twice daily; also offers a half-day kayak tour up the Wailua to Kamokila Village, combined with a hike up to Secret Falls. Cost of basic, 4-hour tour: $50.00 per person ($45.00 children).

Outfitters Kauai. 2827A Poipu Rd. (at Poipu Plaza), Poipu Beach; (808) 742-9667/*www.outfitterskauai.com*. Guided sea kayak tours of the Hule'ia River National Wildlife Refuge, Wailua River, Poipu (south shore) coastline, Na Pali Coast (15-mile paddle), and a Kipu Falls "Zipline Safari," with trips ranging from 2½ hours to all day. Tour cost: Hule'ia River Wildlife refuge tour, $90.00; Wailua River tour, $94.00; South Shore Sea Kayak Tour, $129.00 per person; Na Pali Kayak Adventure, $185.00; and "Zipline Safari," $145.00.

Princeville Ranch Adventures. P.O. Box 224, Hanalei, HI 96714; (808) 826-7669/(888) 955-7669/*www.adventureskauai.com*. Offers 4-hour guided kayak trip to a waterfall on the north shore, with picnic lunch by the pool at the falls. Cost: $94.00.

Surfing, Windsurfing and Waterskiing

Anini Beach Windsurfing. Hanalei; (808) 826-9463. 2- to 3-hour morning and afternoon windsurfing lessons at Anini Beach on the North Shore; also sailboard rentals. Cost: sailboard rentals, $25-$50; lessons, $50-$75.

Hanalei Surf Company. 5-5161 Kuhio Hwy., P.O. Box 790, Hanalei, HI 96714; (808) 826-9000/(866) 426-2534/*www.hana-leisurf.com*. Rentals available, of snorkeling equipment, surfboards and boogie boards; daily and weekly rates. Rental cost: surfboards, $15.00 daily, $65.00 weekly; boogie boards, $5.00 daily, $20.00

weekly, snorkeling gear, $5.00 daily, $20.00 weekly.

Hawaiian Surfing Adventures. P.O. Box 1154, Kilauea, HI 96754; (808) 482-0749/*www.hawaiiansurfingadventures.com*. Surfing lessons, surfboard rentals and guided surfing safaris to the best surf spots on the island at any given time. Cost: 1½- to 2-hour group or private surfing lessons, $55-$75; 1 hour to 1 week surfboard rentals, $10-$75; surfing safaris, $125-$150.

Kauai Waterski. Surf and Kayak Company. 4-356 Kuhio Hwy., Kapa'a, HI 96746; (808) 822-3574/*www.kauaiwaterskisurfand-kayak.com*. Offers surfing lessons and surfboard, bodyboard and snorkeling equipment sales and rentals. Also 4½-hour kayak tours up the Wailua River, and ½-hour and 1-hour waterskiing tows. Cost: surfboard rentals, $10.00 per day, $50.00 per week; kayak tour, $50.00 ($45.00 children); ½-hour waterskiing tow, $65.00; 1-hour tow, $120.00.

Windsurf Kauai. Kilauea; (808) 828-6838. Offers beginner lessons as well as certification courses in windsurfing at Anini Beach; both adult- and kid-size boards are available. Cost of lessons: $60-$75 for 2- to 3-hour lesson.

Golf Courses

Kiahuna Golf Club. 2545 Kiahuna Plantation Dr., Poipu; (808) 742-9595/*www.kiahunagolf.com*. 18-hole, Robert Trent Jones-designed championship course; 6,885 yards, par 70. Green fees (including cart): $90.00 ($50.00 twilight, after 3 p.m.). Facilities include pro shop, club rentals, driving range and lessons; also restaurant and bar on premises.

Kukuiolono Golf Course. 854 Pu'u Rd., Kalaheo; (808) 332-9151. 9-hole course with panoramic views and a Japanese garden in the middle of a fairway; 2,980 yards, par 36. Green fees: $8.00 (cart rental, additional $7.00). Pro shop, club rentals, driving range, restaurant.

Poipu Bay Resort Golf Course. 2250 Ainako St., Poipu; (808) 742-8711/(800) 858-6300/*www.poipubaygolf.com*. Prestigious, 18-hole oceanfront course, designed by Robert Trent Jones, Jr.; par 72, 6,959 yards. Green fees (including cart): $185.00 ($65.00 during twilight hours). Pro shop, club rentals, driving range, restaurant and lounge.

Princeville Resort Golf Courses. At the Princeville Resort, 5-3900 Kuhio Hwy. (56), Princeville; (808) 826-5070/826-5000 (Prince Course)/826-3580 (Makai Course)/(800) 826-1105/*www. princeville.com/play/pvgolf.html*. The resort offers two world-class, Robert Trent Jones-designed courses: the 27-hole *Makai Course*, and the newer, 18-hole *Prince Course*. The *Prince Course* is 7,309 yards, par 72; and the *Makai Course* comprises three 9-hole, par-36 courses—*Makai Ocean*, which is 3,157 yards; *Makai Lakes*, which is 3,149 yards, and the 3,208-yard *Makai Woods*. Green fees (including cart): *Prince Course*, $175.00 ($130.00 for Princeville Hotel guests $85.00 twilight hours); *Makai Course*, $125.00 ($105.00 for Princeville Hotel guests, $85.00 twilight hours). Facilities include pro shop, club rentals, and driving range; also restaurant and lounge.

Wailua Golf Course. 3-5351 Kuhio Hwy., Wailua; (808) 241-6666. 18-hole municipal course; 6,981 yards, par 72. Green fees: $32.00 weekdays, $44.00 weekends, and half price after 3 p.m. (cart rental, additional $16.00). Pro shop, driving range, restaurant and cocktail lounge.

Kauai Lagoons Golf Club. Located adjacent to the Westin Kauai, at 3551 Ho'olaulea Way (off Rice St.)., Lihue; (808) 241-6000/(800) 634-6400/*www.kauailagoonsgolf.com*. Offers two 18-hole, par-72, Jack Nicklaus-designed courses—the *Kiele Course* and the *Mokihana Course*, 7,070 yards and 6,942 yards, respectively. Green fees: *Kiele Course*, $170.00 ($130.00 for hotel guests, $115.00 during afternoon hours); *Mokihana Course*, $125.00 ($75.00 for hotel guests, $75.00 afternoon hours). Pro shop, club rentals, driving range; restaurant and lounge.

Puakea Golf Course. 4150 Nuhou St., Lihue; (808) 245-8756/(866) 773-5554/*www.puakeagolf.com*. Kauai's newest, 18-hole championship course, designed by Robin Nelson. The course is 6,954 yards, par 72, and offers ocean views. Green fees (including cart): $125.00 ($65.00 during twilight hours). Facilities include pro shop, club rentals, driving range, lessons, and restaurant.

Tennis

Kiahuna Tennis Club. 2253 Poipu Rd., Poipu; (808) 742-9533. 10 courts for day use. Court fee: $10.00 per hour. Pro shop and restaurant on premises.

Princeville Tennis Club. Lieopapa Rd., Princeville; (808) 826-9823. 6 courts. Court fee: $12.50 per hour.

Marriott Kauai Beach Club. Kalapaki Beach, 3351 Ho'olauea Way, Lihue; (808) 241-6000/245-5050/(800) 228-3000. 8 courts available for day use; also pro shop, and lessons. Court fee: $10.00 per hour.

Radisson Kauai Beach Resort Tennis Courts. 4331 Kauai Beach Dr., Lihue; (808) 245-1955/(888) 805-3843. 4 courts, including 2 lighted courts for night play. No court fee.

Public Tennis Courts:

Hanapepe Public Tennis Courts, Puolo Rd. (at the Hanapepe Stadium), Hanapepe. 4 courts with lights.

Kalaheo Tennis Courts, Pu'uwai Rd. (at the Kalawai Park), Kalaheo. 2 courts with lights.

Kapa'a Tennis Courts, cnr. Olohena Rd. and Kahau Rd., Kapa'a. 4 courts with lights.

Koloa Tennis Courts, Maluhia Rd. (next to fire station), Koloa. 2 courts, with lights.

Kekaha Tennis Courts, Alae Rd., Kekaha. 2 courts with lights.

Lihue Tennis Court, Hardy St. (next to Kauai War Memorial Convention Hall), Lihue. 2 courts with lights.

Wailua Homelots Tennis Courts, Nounou Rd., Wailua. 4 courts with lights.

Wailua Homestead Park, Kamalu Rd. (Hwy. 581), between mile markers 4 and 5, in Wailua. 4 courts with lights.

Waimea Tennis Courts, Ola Rd., Waimea. 4 courts with lights.

Luaus

Drums of Paradise Luau. At the Hyatt Regency Kauai, Poipu; (808) 742-1234/*www.drumsofparadise.com*. Traditional Hawaiian luau, with lei greeting, hula, crafts demonstrations, and all-you-can-eat buffet. 5.45 p.m.-8 p.m., Thursdays and Sundays. Reservations recommended.

Kauai Aloha Luau. At the Radisson Kauai Beach Resort, 4331 Kauai Beach Dr., Lihue; (877)) 237-7700/ (808) 245-1955/(800) 333-3333/*www.luau-hawaii.com*. Spectacular Polynesian show, including Samoan fire dancers. Also hula dancers and hula lessons, and traditional all-you-can-eat buffet, with kalua pig, Hawaiian sweet potatoes and mai tais. Luaus on Sundays, 5.15-8.00 p.m. Cost: $60.00 adults, $30.00 children. Reservations recommended.

Kauai's Best Luau. At the Aloha Beach Resort, Wailua; (808) (877) 237-7700/*www.luau-hawaii.com*. Traditional luau with Hawaiian music and dance, including the hula. Also Tahitian dances and Samoan Fire Knife Dance. All-you-can-eat buffet. Luaus on Thursdays, 5.15-8.00 p.m. $60.00 adults, $30.00 children. Reservations recommended.

Courtyard by Marriott Kauai Luau. 4-484 Kuhio Hwy. (56), Wailua; (808) 823-0311/*www.tihati.com*. Extravagant, authentic presentation, with traditional Hawaiian food, music and dance. All-you-can-eat buffet. Luaus begin at 6.15 p.m., Tues.-Sun. Cost: $62.00 adults, $30.00 children (6-12). Reservations recommended.

Smith's Tropical Paradise. At the Wailua Marina, Wailua; (808)

821-6895. Popular Polynesian show, in beautiful, tropical setting. Features authentic Hawaiian and Polynesian foods. Begins at 6 p.m., Mon.-Fri. Cost: $60.00 per person. Reservations suggested.

Surf to Sunset Luau. At the Sheraton Kauai, 2440 Ho'onani Rd., Poipu; (808) 742-8200/742-1661/*www.sheratonkauai.com*. Traditional Hawaiian luau, with island entertainment and hula show, and all-you-can-eat Hawaiian feast with kalua pig and a host of island foods and drinks. Luaus begin at 6 p.m. Cost: $68-$80 adults, $34-$40 children (6-12).

Island Events

January

Third and Fourth Weeks. *Kauaian Days*. Two-week cultural celebrations at various locations on the island, honoring Kauai's last reigning monarch, King Kaumuali'i. Events include a parade down Rice St. in Lihue on opening day, cultural displays, Hawaiian crafts and games, and food concessions. Also hula and live entertainment. For a schedule and more information on events and contacts for various events, call (808) 338-0111 or visit *www.kauaiandays.org*.

January-October. *Kauai All-Girls Rodeo*. At the CJM Country Stables in Poipu. Competition series featuring Kauai's cowgirls in rodeo events, including team roping, barrel racing, goat tying, pole bending and steer undecorating. More information at (808) 742-5229/*www.kauairodeo.org*.

February

Third Weekend. *Waimea Town Celebration*. Two-day annual event, held at the Old Waimea Sugar Mill and Waimea Athletic Field, in Waimea. Celebration of Waimea's plantation and *paniolo* heritage. Festivities include games, crafts, musical entertainment and hula dancers, food concessions, canoe races and rodeo events. More information at (808) 335-2824/338-9957/*www.wkbpa.org*. *Captain Cook Caper*. This is part of the "Waimea Town Celebration." Features 2K, 5K and 10K runs through the town of Waimea, drawing approximately 300 participants. Same contact as above, (808) 338-9957.

March

Fourth Week. *Prince Kuhio Celebration.* At the Prince Kuhio Park and the Hyatt Regency Kauai Resort in Poipu. Celebration of Prince Kuhio's birthday. Events include luau and hula performances, exhibits of Hawaiian history and culture, and demonstrations of Hawaiian crafts, including making Ni'ihau shell leis, woodcarving and poi pounding. Also live music and evening concert. More information at (808) 240-6369 or *www.kauaifestivals.com.*

April

Mid-April to August (Sundays). *Polo Matches.* Held at the Kauai Polo Club, across from Anini Beach Park, in Hanalei. Polo matches in tropical setting, every Sunday during season. Matches begin at 3 p.m. More information at (808) 826-4472/823-8888/*www.kauaipoloclub.org.*

Fourth Weekend. *US Team Roping Competition.* Hosted by CJM Country Stables in Poipu. Features rodeo events, with cattle roping competitions drawing top ropers from around the country. Also food concessions. (808) 742-6096/*www.kauaifestivals.com.*

May

First Weekend. *May Day Lei Contest.* Celebration of Hawaiian leis, with an island-wide lei-making competition, held at the Kauai Museum in Lihue, on May 1st every year. Features colorful leis, made from flowers, feathers and shells; also art, crafts and Hawaiian food. (808) 245-6931/*www.kauaimuseum.org. Kauai's World Challenge.* Wailua Beach, Wailua. Individual paddler races and surf-ski relays. More information at (808) 826-5506. *Mother's Day Orchid Show.* At the Kukui Grove Shopping Center. Annual event, featuring hundreds of varieties of orchids on display and available for sale. Also lectures and demonstrations centered around orchid culture. More information at (808) 823-6921.

Second Weekend. *Prince Albert Music Festival.* Princeville Hotel, Princeville. Event features some of the world's foremost classical musicians, along with top Hawaiian musicians. Cost: $15-$90. For reservations and more information, call (808) 826-7546/826-9644; email: *princefound@hotmail.com.*

Fourth Weekend. *Banana Poka Festival.* At Koke'e Museum,

Koke'e. Annual forest-education fair, with mountain music and other entertainment, hikes, exhibits and craft workshops, such as basket weaving. More information as (808) 335-9975/*www.kokee. org*.

Also see *Ongoing Events*.

June

Friday and Saturday Evenings. *O Bon Festival Dances*. Held at the Kapa'a Jodo Mission and various other Buddhist temples throughout the island. Festival held in remembrance of the dead, usually at a different temple each weekend, for 10 weeks. Activities include traditional Japanese folk dances, taiko drumming, food, game and crafts booths. Check local newspapers for a schedule, or contact (808) 822-4319/*www.kauaifestivals.com*.

Saturdays. *Wonder Walk Forest Hikes*. At Koke'e State Park. 2½- to 5-hour guided hikes through upland forest environment and parts of Waimea Canyon, offered every Saturday in June, July and August. Meet at Natural History Museum, hikes depart at 12.15 p.m. Bring water, sunscreen, protective clothing and hiking boots. Pre-registra- tion required. More information at (808) 335-9975/*www.kokee.org*.

Second Weekend. *Kamehameha Day*. Held at the Vidinha Stadium, off Rice St., in Lihue. Cultural festival celebrating the birthday of Kamehameha the Great. Features a parade with colorful floral floats and mounted horses. Also Hawaiian dance and music, cultural displays, arts and crafts, and food concessions. Call (808) 651-9953/*www.kauaifestivals.com*.

Also see *Ongoing Events*.

July

Fourth of July. *Concert in the Sky* at Vidinha Stadium in Lihue. Annual fundraiser for the Kauai Hospice; features live entertain- ment, food concessions, children's activities, a silent auction and an Independence Day fireworks show. Events begin at 3 p.m. Cost: $10-$13 adults, $7.00 children (6-12). For information and advance tickets, call (808) 245-7277/*www.kauaihospice.org*.

Fourth Week. *Koloa Plantation Days*. Week-long celebration, commemorating the birth of Hawaii's sugar industry in Koloa. Ac- tivities take place at various locations in Koloa and Poipu. Features a colorful parade through the town of Koloa, guided walks through historic Old Koloa Town, traditional Hawaiian games and entertain- ment, including ethnic songs and dances. Also arts and crafts fair, food concessions, rodeo, canoe races, and golf and tennis tournaments. More information at (808) 822-0734/*www.koloaplantation-days.com*.

Also see *Ongoing Events*.

August

Fourth Weekend. *Kauai County Farm Bureau Fair*. At the Vidinha Stadium in Lihue. Features a livestock show and petting zoo; also games and rides, arts and crafts, exhibits, floral demonstrations, food concessions, and live entertainment. For more information, call the Kauai Farm Bureau at (808) 639-8432.

Also see *Ongoing Events*.

September

Third Week. *Kauai Mokihana Festival*. At various locations throughout the island. Week-long celebration of the arts on Kauai. Activities include a composer's contest and concert, arts and crafts fair, folk art workshops, benefit concert, women's and men's hula competitions. Call (808) 822-2166/*www.mokihana.kauai.net*.

All Month. *Aloha Festival*. Month-long festival with events staged all around the island. Features Hawaiian pageantry, and demonstrations in lei making, poi pounding, coconut husking, coconut weaving and Hawaiian-style quilting; also parades, arts and crafts, food, island fruit tasting, canoe races, and entertainment—including original Hawaiian music and hula dancers. For a schedule of events in Kauai, contact the Aloha Festivals office at (808) 245-8508 or visit *www.alohafestivals.com*.

Also see *Ongoing Events*.

October

First Weekend. *Eo e Emalani i Alaka'i Festival*. Held at the Koke'e State Park, Kekaha. Annual outdoor festival, honoring Queen Emma. Features hula and Hawaiian music; also procession, cultural exhibits and craft demonstrations. More information at (808) 335-9975/*www.kokee.org*. *Coconut Festival*. At the Kapa'a State Beach Park. A two-day Coconut Coast celebration, featuring live performances by local and Honolulu-based performers. Cooking demonstrations using coconuts, food concessions, workshops, cultural exhibits, games, crafts, and hula. More information at (808) 651-3273/*www.kauaifestivals.com*.

November

Third Week. *Hawaii International Film Festival.* Free screenings of cross-cultural films by award-winning film makers from Asia, the Pacific, Europe, Latin America and the US. Also seminars and workshops. Also short films competition for local, amateur filmmakers. More information at (800) 752-8193/*www.hiff.org.*

Fourth Week. *PGA Grand Slam of Golf.* At Poipu Bay Resort Golf Course, adjacent to the Hyatt Regency Kauai. Winners of this year's major PGA championships will compete for a purse of $1 million. Fore more information, call (808) 742-8711/742-6300; for ticket information, call (800) 742-8258/*www.pga.com.*

December

First Weekend. *Kauai Museum Christmas Craft Fair.* Kauai Museum, Lihue. Two-day craft fair, featuring local craftspeople. Also wreath-making contest and silent auction. More information at (808) 245-6931/*www.kauaimuseum.org.*

Third Weekend. *Waimea Lighted Christmas Parade.* Staged in the center of Waimea on the last Saturday before Christmas. Annual holiday celebration with a parade of lighted and decorated floats through the center of town. Also local food and refreshments, and live entertainment. More information at (808) 335-2824/338-9957/ *www.wkbpa.org.*

Ongoing Events

January-October. *Kauai All-Girls Rodeo.* At the CJM Country Stables in Poipu. Competition series featuring Kauai's cowgirls in rodeo events, including team roping, barrel racing, goat tying, pole bending and steer undecorating. More information at (808) 742-5229/*www.kauairodeo.org.*

Mid-April to August (Sundays). *Polo Matches.* Held at the Kauai Polo Club, across from Anini Beach Park, in Hanalei. Polo matches in tropical setting, every Sunday during season. Matches begin at 3 p.m. More information at (808) 826-4472/823-8888/*www.kauaipoloclub.org.*

June-August (Friday and Saturday Evenings). *O Bon Festival Dances.* Held at the Kapa'a Jodo Mission and various other Buddhist temples throughout the island. Festival held in remembrance of the dead, usually at a different temple each weekend, for 10 weeks. Activities include traditional Japanese folk dances, taiko drumming, food, game and crafts booths. Check local newspapers for a schedule, or contact (808) 822-4319/*www.kauaifestivals.com*.

June-August (Saturdays). *Wonder Walk Forest Hikes.* At Koke'e State Park. 2½- to 5-hour guided hikes through upland forest environment and parts of Waimea Canyon, offered every Saturday in June, July and August. Meet at Natural History Museum, hikes depart at 12.15 p.m. Bring water, sunscreen, protective clothing and hiking boots. Pre-registration required. More information at (808) 335-9975/*www.kokee.org*

Year-round. *Sugar Plantation Tours.* Gay & Robinson Kaumakani Plantation. Guided bus and walking tours of the plantation. Two-hour tour includes historical information, as well as an overview of the day-to-day operations. Tours at 9 a.m. and 1 p.m., Mon.-Fri. Tour cost: $30.00 adults, $21.00 children. Reservations required. Reservations and more information at (808) 335-2824/*www.gan-drtours-kauai.com*.

Year-round. *Friday Art Night.* Hanapepe Town. Every Friday evening, from 6-9 p.m., artists and craftspeople exhibit and demonstrate their work. Cultural displays. Live entertainment. Also local galleries, shops and cafes remain open. More information at (808) 246-2111/*www.kauaifestivals.com*.

Year-round. *Old Waimea Sugar Plantation Walking Tour.* One-hour tours of the plantation neighborhood of the Old Waimea Sugar Plantation in Waimea. Learn about the architecture of this historic area, as well as the immigrants who came from all over the world to work in the sugar industry. Guided tours are offered at 9 a.m. on Tues., Thurs., and Sat. Tour cost: $10.00, $5.00 children. For reservations or more information, call (808) 335-2824/*www.gandrtours-kauai.com*.

Year-round. *National Tropical Botanical Garden Tours - McBryde and Allerton Gardens.* Guided tours of Allerton Garden, with its "landscaped rooms" featuring plants, trees, sculpture and water features, are offered four times daily, Tues.-Sat. Tours of McBryde Garden, which features rare native plants, historic buildings, and a turtle nesting area on the beach, are offered on Mondays only. Tours begin at the visitor center, across from Spouting Horn, in Poipu. Reservations are required for all tours; call (808) 742-2623.

Year-round. *Hula Shows.* Free hula shows are offered at the following locations: *Coconut Marketplace*, 5-5.30 p.m. on Wednesdays, (808) 822-3641/*www.coconutmarketplace.com*; *Hyatt Regency Kauai Resort*, 7-8 p.m. Tuesdays and Saturdays, (808) 742-1234; *Princeville Hotel*, 6.30-7 p.m. on Sundays; (808) 826-9644.

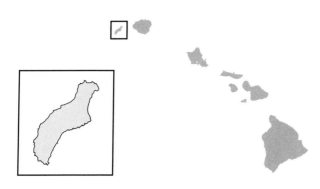

Ni'ihau | A Glimpse of the Island

Ni'ihau is Hawaii's last holdout. It is privately owned and off limits to both visitors and Hawaiians not resident on the island. And that is how it has been for the past 140-plus years.

The island is 18 miles long and 6 miles wide (72 square miles in area), the smallest of the eight major Hawaiian islands. It is largely flat and arid, with an average annual rainfall of 25-30 inches. Its highest point is Paniau, elevation 1,281 feet. But the most surprising thing about it is that despite the dearth of rainfall it boasts Hawaii's largest freshwater lake, Halali'i, which has a surface area of almost 850 acres.

Ni'ihau lies approximately 17½ miles west-southwest of Kauai, the farthest away from the other six major Hawaiian islands, making it virtually an outpost of the island chain.

Background

In 1864, Elizabeth Sinclair, a Scottish woman traveling with her family from New Zealand, came upon Ni'ihau and purchased it from King Kamehameha V for a reported $10,000, to raise sheep and cattle. Today, cattle ranching remains the principal industry on the island, and the Sinclair descendants, the Robinson family, continue to own the island and perpetuate the tradition of excluding outsiders from it, preserving it as the last vestige of the Hawaiian way of life.

Ni'ihau has a population of approximately 220, the majority of it concentrated on the island's west shore, in its principal population center, Pu'uwai. The island has no electricity—refrigerators and television sets are powered by generators—or plumbing or telephones, and the island's catchment system is used to collect water.

NI'IHAU | The Forbidden Isle

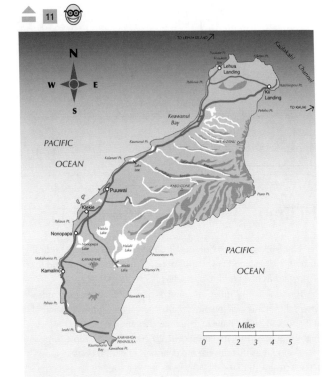

NI'IHAU

The primary language spoken on Ni'ihau is Hawaiian, with English relegated to secondary language status. The island has one school that goes up to eighth grade, beyond which students must transfer to a school on Kauai to continue their education.

Ni'ihau's residents are employed either on the island's cattle ranch or on the Gay & Robinson sugar plantation at Makaweli, on the west shore of Kauai. Island residents are allowed to come and go, to and from the island, at their choosing; however, once they leave the island as their place of residence, they may only return to visit family members still residing on the island.

Ni'ihau is best known for its seashells that are unique and beautiful, and nowhere else to be found in the Pacific. The shells are used to make leis that are among the most treasured (and most expensive) in Hawaii. The island's hand-woven mats are also highly prized, both for their design and craftsmanship.

Touring the Island

  See Map 11 for Orientation

The best—and only—way to see Ni'ihau is on an organized helicopter tour offered by the Robinson family (who own the island) interests.

The tours are approximately 3 hours long and cover much of the island—with the notable exception of the village of Pu'uwai. They include a 20-minute recess on the south shore of the island, and a 1-hour stop on the north shore. Refreshments are provided enroute as well as at the stops, and visitors are afforded brief beachcombing opportunities on the island's beaches. Cost of the tour is $200.00. For reservations and more information, contact *Ni'ihau Helicopters*, Makaweli, at (808) 335-3500.

NI'IHAU | The Forbidden Isle

HAWAIIAN REEF FISH

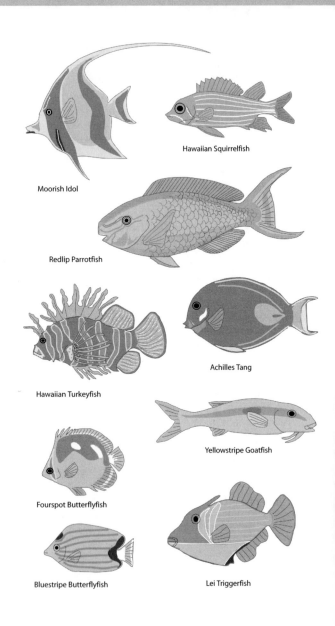

Moorish Idol

Hawaiian Squirrelfish

Redlip Parrotfish

Hawaiian Turkeyfish

Achilles Tang

Yellowstripe Goatfish

Fourspot Butterflyfish

Bluestripe Butterflyfish

Lei Triggerfish

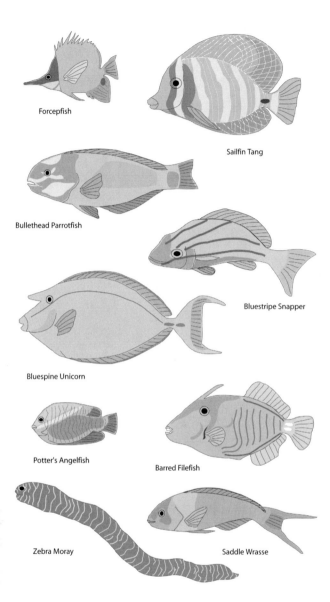

Forcepfish

Sailfin Tang

Bullethead Parrotfish

Bluestripe Snapper

Bluespine Unicorn

Potter's Angelfish

Barred Filefish

Zebra Moray

Saddle Wrasse

HAWAIIAN LEIS

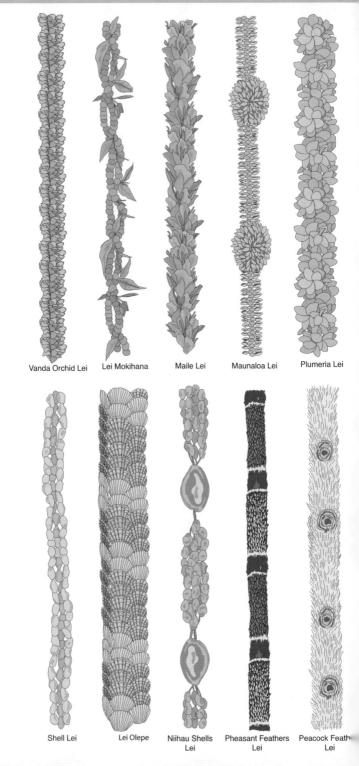

Vanda Orchid Lei

Lei Mokihana

Maile Lei

Maunaloa Lei

Plumeria Lei

Shell Lei

Lei Olepe

Niihau Shells Lei

Pheasant Feathers Lei

Peacock Feath Lei

HAWAIIAN GLOSSARY

The Hawaiian language, in its simplicity, contains only seven consonants—H, K, L, M, N, P, W—and five vowels—A, E, I, O and U. All words—and syllables—end in a vowel, and all syllables begin with a consonant. The vowels, typically, are each pronounced separately—i.e., a'a is pronounced "ah-ah," and e'e is pronounced "ay-ay"; the only exceptions are the diphthong double vowels—ai, pronounced "eye," and *au,* pronounced "ow." The consonants, on the other hand, are never doubled.

Hawaiian consonants are pronounced similar to those in English, with the notable exception of W, which is sometimes pronounced as "V," when it begins the last syllable of the word. Hawaiian vowels are pronounced as follows: A- "uh," as in among; E - "ay," as in day; I - "ee," as in deep; O - "oh," as in no; U - "oo," as in blue.

For travellers to the Hawaiian islands, the following is a glossary of some commonly used words in the Hawaiian language.

a'a — rough, crumbling lava.

ae — yes.

ahi — tuna fish.

ahupua'a — pie-shaped land division, extending from the mountains to the sea.

aikane — friend.

alanui — road, or path.

ali'i — a Hawaiian chief or nobleman.

aloha — love, or affection; traditional Hawaiian greeting, meaning both welcome and farewell.

anu — cold, cool.

a'ole — no.

auwe — alas!

awawa — valley.

hala — the pandanus tree, the leaves of which are used to make baskets and mats.

hale — house.

hale pule — church; house of worship.

hana — work.

hahana — hot, warm.

haole — foreigner; frequently used to refer to a Caucasian.

hapa — half, as in *hapa-haole,* or half Caucasian.

haupia — coconut cream pudding, often served at a *luau.*

heiau — an ancient Hawaiian place of worship; shrine, temple.

holoholo — to go for a walk; also to ride or sail.

honi — a kiss; also, to kiss.

hui — a group, society, or assembly of people.

hukilau — a communal fishing party, in which everyone helpspull in the fishing nets.

hula — traditional Hawaiian dance of storytelling.

imu — underground oven, used for roasting pigs for *luaus.*

ipo — sweetheart, or lover.

ka'ahele — a tour.

ka'ao — legend.

kahuna — priest, minister, sorcerer, prophet.

kai — the sea.

kakahiaka — morning.

kama'aina — native-born, or local.

kanaka — man, usually of Hawaiian descent.

kane — male, husband.

kapu —taboo, forbidden; derived from the Tongan word, *tabu.*

keiki — child; a male child is known as *keikikane,* and a female child, *keikiwahine.*

kiawe — Algaroba tree, with fern-like leaves and sharp, long thorns, usually found in dry areas near the coast. Kiawe wood is used to make charcoal for fuel. The tree was introduced to Hawaii in the 1820s.

koa — native Hawaiian tree, prized for its wood which was used by early Hawaiians to craft canoes, spears and surfboards. Koa wood is now used to make fine furniture.

kokua — help.

kona — leeward side of island; frequently used to describe storms and winds, such as *kona* storm or *kona* wind. Also, south.

ko'olau — windward side of island.

kukui — Candlenut tree, characteristic in its yellow and green foliage, generally found in the valleys. Kukui nuts are also used in *leis.* Kukui is Hawaii's state tree.

kuleana — home site, or homestead; also responsibility, or one's business.

kupuna — grandparent.

lamalama — torch fishing

lanai — porch, veranda, balcony.

lani — the sky, or heaven

laulau — wrapped package; generally used to describe bundles of pork, fish or beef, served with *taro* shoots, wrapped in *ti* or banana leaves, and steamed.

lei — garland, wreath, or necklace of flowers.

lilikoi — passion fruit.

limu — seaweed.

luau — traditional Hawaiian feast.

mahalo — thanks, or thank you.

mahi-mahi — dolphin.

maile — native vine with shiny, fragrant leaves used in leis.

makahiki hou — New Year; *hauoli makahiki hou,* Happy New Year.

make — to die, or dead.

makai — toward the ocean, or seaward.

malihini — stranger, newcomer.

mana — supernatural power.

manu — bird.

mauka — toward the mountain, or inland.

mauna — mountain.

mele — song, chant.

menehune — Hawaii's legendary little people, ingenious and hardworking, who worked only at night, building fishponds, heiaus, irrigation ditches and roads, many of which remain today.

moana — the ocean; open sea.

mo'o — lizard, dragon, serpent.

mu'umu'u — long, loose, traditional Hawaiian dress.

nani — beautiful.

nui — big.

ohana — family.

ono — delicious.

pakalolo — marijuana.

palapala — book; also printing.

pali — cliff; also plural, cliffs.

paniolo — Hawaiian cowboy.

pau — finished, all done.

poi — a purplish paste made from pounded and cooked *taro* roots; staple of Hawaiian diet.

puka — hole, opening.

pupu — appetizer, snack, hors d'oeuvre.

pupule — crazy; insane.

tapa — cloth made from beaten bark, often used in Hawaiian clothing.

taro — broad-leafed plant with starch root, used to make poi; staff of life of early Hawaiians, introduced to the islands by the first Polynesians.

ti — broad-leafed plant, brought to Hawaii by early Polynesian immigrants. *Ti* leaves are used for wrapping food as well as offerings to the gods.

waha — mouth; *waha nui, a* big mouth.

wahine — female, woman, wife.

wai — fresh water.

wiki — to hurry; *wikiwiki,* hurry up.